Positiv

Find happiness and achieve your goals through the power of positive thought

Gill Hasson

CAPSTONE
A Wiley Brand

This edition first published 2017

© 2017 Gill Hasson

Registered office
John Wiley & Sons Ltd, The Atrium, Southern Gate, Chichester, West Sussex, PO19 8SQ, United Kingdom

For details of our global editorial offices, for customer services and for information about how to apply for permission to reuse the copyright material in this book please see our website at www.wiley.com.

Wiley publishes in a variety of print and electronic formats and by print-on-demand. Some material included with standard print versions of this book may not be included in e-books or in print-on-demand. If this book refers to media such as a CD or DVD that is not included in the version you purchased, you may download this material at http://booksupport.wiley.com. For more information about Wiley products, visit www.wiley.com.

Designations used by companies to distinguish their products are often claimed as trademarks. All brand names and product names used in this book and on its cover are trade names, service marks, trademarks or registered trademarks of their respective owners. The publisher and the book are not associated with any product or vendor mentioned in this book. None of the companies referenced within the book have endorsed the book.

Limit of Liability/Disclaimer of Warranty: While the publisher and author have used their best efforts in preparing this book, they make no representations or warranties with respect to the accuracy or completeness of the contents of this book and specifically disclaim any implied warranties of merchantability or fitness for a particular purpose. It is sold on the understanding that the publisher is not engaged in rendering professional services and neither the publisher nor the author shall be liable for damages arising herefrom. If professional advice or other expert assistance is required, the services of a competent professional should be sought.

Library of Congress Cataloging-in-Publication Data

Names: Hasson, Gill, author.
Title: Positive thinking : find happiness and achieve your goals through the power of positive thought / Gill Hasson.
Description: Chichester, West Sussex, UK : John Wiley & Sons, 2017. | Includes index.
Identifiers: LCCN 2016029047| ISBN 9780857086839 (pbk.)
Subjects: LCSH: Attitude (Psychology) | Positive psychology. | Self-esteem.
Classification: LCC BF327 .H387 2017 | DDC 150.19/88–dc23 LC record available at https://lccn.loc.gov/2016029047

A catalogue record for this book is available from the British Library.

ISBN 978-0-857-08683-9 (pbk)
ISBN 978-0-857-08692-1 (ebk) ISBN 978-0-857-08691-4 (ebk)

Cover design: Wiley

Set in 12/15 pt SabonLTStd by Aptara Inc., New Delhi, India

Printed in Great Britain by TJ International Ltd, Padstow, Cornwall, UK

Contents

Introduction

What do you want? Why do you think positive thinking might help?

Perhaps you want to start your own business, change your job or career, start a relationship, improve a relationship, travel the world. Perhaps you simply want to feel happier and more positive each day.

Maybe you need some positivity to help you cope with a disappointment, setback or even a trauma or tragedy.

Whatever it is, you may have decided that things need to improve and that what could help would be a more positive perspective and approach. You're right; a positive perspective and approach *can* help.

But is there really power in positive thinking? Yes.

The fact is, if you're not a positive thinker – if you don't have a positive attitude – there's not much that can make up for it. Money, education, talent and opportunities are all well and good but without positive thinking you can't really make the most of them. Other people can't be positive for you. They can be supportive and encouraging but then it's over to you.

There simply is no substitute for having your own positive attitude. It gives you the motivation, energy and ability to succeed, it enables you to be happy and keeps you going through the toughest times.

A positive attitude is the difference maker. So how can you get this difference maker in your life? This book will explain how.

Part 1 introduces you to the concepts of positive and negative thinking. It explains that what you think and say to yourself can have quite an impact on what you can and can't do. Think positively and you'll feel able to manage and do well. Let negative thoughts take a hold, and you're likely to feel overwhelmed and powerless.

So why, if negative thinking is so unhelpful to us, do we think in negative ways? Chapter 1 explains why. And there's a questionnaire for you to complete, which will give you an idea of just how negative or positive you currently are.

If you are more inclined to think in negative ways, the good news is that once you're more aware of your negative thoughts, you're in a better position to disempower them. In Chapter 2 you'll learn how to challenge negative thoughts and choose more helpful, positive ways of thinking.

You'll also learn about a new approach – a mindful approach – which suggests that instead of challenging negative thoughts, you simply accept and let go of those thoughts and turn your attention, time and energy to the outcomes you would really prefer.

Some people claim that positive thinking is unrealistic; that you can't get what you want in life simply by being positive and optimistic and suppressing or ignoring the negative aspects of life. It's true; that is unrealistic.

It's unrealistic because positive thinking is more than a way to manage your thoughts – positive thinking is about what you think and what you do. It involves being proactive. Positive thinking needs to be followed by positive action. Chapter 3 explains this. It explains what you can do to achieve your goals and get what you want and it explains how positive thinking can help support you in your efforts.

Whatever it is you want to do, though, whatever goals you're aiming to achieve, it's quite possible that despite your good intentions, you either can't get yourself started or you've got started but now you're flagging. Part 2 begins by explaining, in Chapter 4, a number of ways that you can develop your willpower and motivation and keep going.

With positive thinking, what you're aiming for is to make it a habit. A positive habit. Chapter 5 has a range of ideas, tips and techniques for establishing a positive mindset. You'll discover that the more you train your brain to think positively, the more likely you'll have helpful, positive thoughts and beliefs that will soon become your normal way of thinking.

Continuing with the theme of developing and maintaining positive thinking, Chapter 6 looks at the links between positive thinking, self-esteem and confidence. When your self-esteem is high, your thoughts and beliefs about yourself are positive; you feel good about yourself and you're more likely to believe that you can do things, things can turn out well and you can cope with setbacks. It's a helpful, positive dynamic where each aspect feeds into the other. Chapter 6 suggests a variety of ways that you can build your self-esteem and confidence and tap into that positive dynamic.

So far, then, so good. But what if you're currently facing challenges and setbacks? What if you've experienced trauma and even tragedy? How can positive thinking be of any real practical help?

So much of how we handle problems depends on how we make meaning out of our experiences.

Finding something positive in adversity doesn't mean denying how difficult or devastating the situation is, but it can help prevent you from being overwhelmed by the awfulness of it.

The final section of this book – Part 3 – looks at the role of positive thinking in a number of difficult and challenging situations.

Chapter 7 looks at managing, amongst other things, disappointment, guilt, regret and tragedy. It emphasizes the need for courage – the bravest, most intrepid form of positive thinking – and explains that, whatever the circumstances, you can see possibilities and find hope in the most difficult of times.

And finally, Chapter 8 looks at the sort of negative mindsets that can cause you stress and hold you back. It explains how to free yourself from, for example, a fear of failure and the unrealistic expectations that can often come with being a perfectionist.

The same principles of positive thinking – let go of negativity and instead focus on the positive – apply throughout Part 3. You'll find that they're emphasized as a way of dealing with the times that you might be inclined to negatively compare yourself with others. A key piece of advice here is to see other people as role models to learn from and be an inspiration to you rather than see others as people who are 'better' or have more than you.

In fact, throughout the book you will read stories of people who have used positive thinking to achieve their goals and overcome difficulties. Hopefully, their stories will inspire you; inspire you to view yourself, your abilities and experiences in a positive light and to approach life and its challenges with a positive outlook.

In the words of the writer Stephen King: 'You can, you should, and if you're brave enough to start, you will.'

So let's get started!

PART 1
Positive Thinking and Positive Action

1
You Are What You Think

Positive thinking vs. negative thinking

Positive thinking will let you do everything better than negative thinking will. Think positively and you're likely to enjoy positive results. Negative thinking, on the other hand, can lead to outcomes you'd rather not have. Negative thinking undermines your confidence. It contributes to indecision. It defeats you. It beats you. It creates the 'bad luck' that you'll later lament.

Think positively and you'll feel able to manage and do well. Think negatively and you're likely to feel overwhelmed and powerless. What you think and say to yourself can have quite an impact on what you can and can't do, as shown by this simple exercise. Try it for yourself. You'll need another person to help.

Part 1:

- Ask the other person to stand and extend their dominant arm out horizontally, at shoulder level so that their arm is parallel with the floor.

- Ask them to think of a time when they failed at something – a test or exam or job interview, for example. Then ask them to think negative thoughts about themselves: 'I'm weak. I'm not as clever as other people. I'm hopeless. I'm pathetic, I'm not good at anything. I can't do this.'
- Ask the person to continue thinking the negative things. Tell them you are going to stand behind them and attempt to pull their dominant arm down to their side. Ask them to resist you pulling their arm down.

Part 2:

- Now, ask the person to hold their dominant arm up again at the shoulders, parallel to the floor.
- This time, ask them to think of a time when they achieved something, succeeded and did well at something – passed a test or exam, got offered the job, did well in a sport, for example. Then ask them to think of positive things about themselves: 'I try my best. I can do well. I feel good about myself. I am a good person. I am strong. I can do this.'
- Ask them to repeat the positive statements to themselves while you attempt to pull their arm down to their side. Ask them to resist the pull.

Typically, in the first part of the exercise, the person's arm is more likely to give way to your pull. Negativity overwhelms them and it's not easy for them to be strong. However, when the person's thoughts are positive, their body has the ability to resist the force that's pulling their arm down. They are more likely to stay strong and resist your pull.

So what does this little experiment prove? It shows us the power of our thoughts over our bodies. When we think negative thoughts, we tend to zap our strength. When we have positive thoughts, we become stronger and are more in control.

You are what you think. And what you think, you are.

It's important to know, though, that neither negative thinking nor positive thinking is more real or true than the other. Either way of thinking could be real or true. But what does make one way of thinking more real is the one you choose to think and believe. As Shakespeare said, 'For there is nothing either good or bad, but thinking makes it so.'

Your thoughts can be understood as your 'self-talk' or your 'inner voice'. Your self-talk provides you with a running commentary rather like the constant text at the bottom of a 24-hour news channel. This self-talk directs your thinking and shapes your beliefs, expectations and actions.

Self-talk has a way of creating its own reality. Telling yourself you can do something can help it happen. Telling yourself you *can't* do something can make it more likely to be true. And because your brain speaks with your own voice, whatever it says, it feels real and it feels true.

To a greater or lesser extent, we simply accept particular beliefs and ways of thinking. That's all well and good if those thoughts are helpful and constructive. It's not so good if those ways of thinking are negative and produce thoughts and feelings that are unhelpful and self-defeating.

Positive intentions of negative thinking

So if positive thinking is the most helpful, beneficial way to think, why do we think in negative ways? Let's start by trying to understand this.

Negative ways of thinking are an aspect of emotions such as fear, worry, anxiety, disappointment, guilt, shame, regret, resentment and jealousy. Often, these emotions include thoughts such as 'I can't do that', 'I'm scared', 'It's not fair', 'I'm such an idiot', 'It's *his* fault', 'It's *her* fault', 'Nothing ever goes right for me' and 'I wish I hadn't done that.'

We usually think of emotions like fear, worry, disappointment etc. as 'negative emotions'. Why? Because they make us feel bad. And yet, these emotions, like all other emotions, do actually have a positive intent.

Take, for example, the emotion of guilt. Typically, the thoughts that accompany guilt are 'I've screwed up, I shouldn't have done that, it's my fault. I feel bad about what I did.'

How can this way of thinking be positive? Well, the positive intent of guilt is to prompt you to recognize your wrongdoing and then to think about and take action to put right or make up for what you did wrong.

If, though, when you feel guilty you simply wallow in your guilt, beat yourself up about what you did wrong or try and suppress or deny how you feel, then your thoughts and actions (or lack of action) remain negative. Those thoughts and actions or inactions do you no good whatsoever.

The positive intentions of 'negative' emotions act in the same way as the positive intention of physical pain. If, for example, you touch something really hot, the pain makes you pull away. It feels bad, but the positive intention of that pain is to protect you. It's the same with emotional pain; it can prompt you to take positive action.

What about a difficult emotion such as regret? How can that be positive? The positive intent of regret is to prompt you to learn from what you now wish you had or hadn't done; to behave differently in future. Regret is only negative when you are stuck in regret; you allow it to keep you there and leave you feeling defeated and hopeless. But it's not the emotion that's negative, it's your thinking and lack of positive response!

Furthermore, the fact that you know that emotions such as guilt and regret make you feel bad can actually motivate you, too. They can motivate you *not* to do something that could result in you feeling guilty or regretful.

Narrow perspectives

Emotions such as guilt, fear, anger, sadness and regret narrow your perspective and your thinking. There is a good reason for this; narrowed thinking focuses your attention on the 'negative' situation so that it becomes the *only* thing you can think about in order that you take action. Positive action. Again, just like putting your hand on something hot, all your attention is focused on it, and your response is positive (and quick!).

Supposing, for example, you're anxious about a test or an exam. The positive intent of anxiety is to focus your thoughts on what you need to revise. It starts to work against you, though, if the anxiety overwhelms you.

Or, supposing one Friday evening you notice a mole on your arm that seems different. You're worried about it. Worry forces you to think about little else over the weekend other than getting to see a doctor on Monday. It's annoying that you can think of little else, but the fact that you are so preoccupied makes it likely you'll go and see the doctor and get the mole checked out.

Another example of an emotion that narrows and focuses your thinking is sadness. Sadness helps you to slow down enough to take in and adjust to your loss.

Emotions such as sadness, anxiety, worry and guilt might not feel good yet they do have beneficial aspects if you respond to them positively. If you don't act positively on those emotions, if you let them overwhelm you, they can contract and distort your world and keep you feeling bad.

In contrast, 'positive' emotions such as hope, compassion and happiness and their associated positive thoughts, can expand your world and the possibilities in it.

Broad perspectives

Psychologist Barbara Fredrickson's research at the University of Carolina shows that positive emotions broaden your sense of possibilities and open your mind, which in turn allows you to see more possibilities and options in a range of situations in your life.

In an experiment by Fredrickson, groups of people were shown different film clips. The first two groups were shown clips that created feelings of contentment and joy. The last two groups were shown clips that provoked feelings of fear and anger. Afterwards, each participant was asked to imagine themselves in a situation where similar negative or positive feelings would arise and to write down as many ways as they could think of that they could respond.

Participants who had seen images of fear and anger wrote down a few responses. Meanwhile, the participants who saw images of joy and contentment wrote down a significantly higher number of actions that they would take.

A University of Toronto study even suggests that what we *see* can be affected by a positive or negative outlook; that positive or negative thinking can change the way our visual cortex – the part of the brain responsible for processing visual information – operates. The study showed that when in a positive mood, our visual cortex takes in more information, while negative moods result in tunnel vision. It would appear that seeing the world through rose-coloured glasses is more than a metaphor!

Positive emotions and their associated positive thoughts open you up to new ideas and new experiences and possibilities. You feel positive about situations and other people. Ten years ago Lou worked for a local government authority. Here, he explains how his perspective differed from that of his colleague, Ned:

I was offered redundancy from my job. Although it wasn't a brilliant redundancy package, I took it.

Telling my friend Ned about it, he thought I was mad to take redundancy; I had two children and my wife was expecting another child. I explained to Ned how free I felt and I told him about my plans to start an online greetings card business.

Ned still thought I was mad; all he could see were the risks. But my view of the world was one of opportunity and new horizons. Of course I realized it wasn't going to be easy but I would be free from the rat race, I would be my own boss, my time would be more flexible, and I would get to see my wife and children a lot more than I had in the past. I was excited about the possibilities opening up to me. And if it didn't work out I would do whatever it took to get back into employment.

Ned didn't understand. He told me that for him, the security of a full-time job was the most important thing. He said that even though he really didn't enjoy his job – it was stressful, he hated his boss and he often worked long hours – he couldn't see any other way. He felt trapped.

Well, as it turned out, I worked at my business for three years and made a reasonable living from it. And I got to spend a lot of time with the children. I eventually sold the business because my wife was made redundant and we figured I'd have a better chance of getting a well-paid employed job. She had also reached a point where *she* wanted to spend more time at home.

Lou's positive thinking reflects an open mind and broadens his ideas, thoughts and actions whereas Ned's negative thinking limits and narrows his world, his opportunities and choices.

Positive thinking brings hope; the feeling that what you want *can* happen or that events *can* turn out for the best. Negative thinking creates a spiral of unhelpful thoughts and difficult feelings. Even when good things happen, negative thinkers tend to see the negative aspects of a situation.

Of course, everybody's view of the world is different, but if you think life is mostly good, you'll notice opportunities and good things in your life; if you think life is difficult, you will find obstacles and difficulties in life.

How positive are you?

Are you inclined to be a negative thinker or are you more of a positive thinker? Do you know what sort of events and situations are more likely to trigger a negative or positive response from you? Below is a range of situations. Read each statement and tick whichever way of thinking or behaving you'd be most likely to take.

1. If I had to pull out of going to an important event with a friend and I felt guilty about it:
   a) I'd think of a way to make it up to her.
   b) I'd know she was annoyed with me and so I'd avoid her until I thought she'd forgotten about it.
2. If someone – friend, family member, colleague – lets me know they need to speak with me about something, I think:
   a) I wonder what this might be about?
   b) I wonder what the problem is? I wonder what I've done wrong.
3. If I was involved in a work project with other people who were not getting on and not working well together I'd most likely think:
   a) We can find a way to sort it out, there has to be a solution that will make things easier for everybody.
   b) This is never going to change – it's our manager's fault – he should've known we wouldn't all get on. Why did I have to be involved with this?

4. Something unexpected comes up which forces you to change your holiday plans. You think:
   a) How am I going to work round this? What are my options?
   b) Why does this *always* happen to me? My plans are all ruined.
5. Someone congratulates you on a piece of work you've done. You say:
   a) Thanks. I'm pleased with what I did.
   b) Thanks, but it wasn't that good. And then you tell them about the aspects that didn't go so well.
6. At work, you are asked to join a team working on an interesting project. You know that the first person to be asked to join the team was unavailable. You think:
   a) Great! This will be an interesting opportunity and it'll be my chance to show what I can do.
   b) They only asked me because the other person couldn't do it. It wouldn't have occurred to them to ask me first.
7. In elections:
   a) I vote for who I think could make a difference; the person I believe will actually get things done.
   b) There's absolutely no point in voting. Things *never* change, *all* politicians are rubbish, and anyway, my vote won't make any difference whatsoever.
8. Your company plans to dismiss 10% of its workforce on grounds of redundancy. Your reaction to the news:

(Continued)

a) I'm going to start thinking about what I might do next; I'll start finding out what other opportunities there might be.

b) It's bound to be me. It's not fair.

9. You trip over and twist your ankle. You think:

a) Oh no! Still, it could've been worse, at least I didn't break my ankle.

b) That'll teach me! I *knew* I shouldn't have sneaked off work today; I *thought* something would go wrong. It's my punishment.

10. When choosing from the menu at a restaurant:

a) I usually find it quite easy to decide what to eat.

b) I often regret my choice and wish I'd chosen something else.

11. You do better than you expected to in a test or exam. You think

a) That's great!

b) I don't know how that happened. It was a fluke.

12. You work for a small company that's rapidly expanding. Your boss is leaving – you'd love her job. You:

a) Ask her advice about applying for her job.

b) Decide you can't say anything – you'll have to wait to be asked to apply.

13. You have to be at work at 9:00am. It is 8:45am and you're still waiting in a traffic jam. You think:

a) I need to call and let work know that I'm running late. At least that important meeting isn't till 9:30am.

b) I shouldn't have taken this route! Now the whole day is going to turn out wrong.

14. You've always wanted to work part time so that you can write a novel/train as a singer/yoga teacher. Now, thanks to your partner's recent pay rise and their encouragement, you can just about afford to do it. You:
    a) Start making plans.
    b) Dismiss the idea. Supposing the novel is crap, you are no good at singing or no one comes to your yoga classes?

15. You have to drive somewhere new. You're anxious about getting lost. You think:
    a) I'll need to plan my route; how to get there and what breaks to make.
    b) I just know I'll get lost. I'll get stressed. I won't know where I'm going or what I'm doing.

16. You tell a friend something personal and although you've asked her not to, she tells another person. You:
    a) Talk to her about it and explain how let down and upset you feel and ask her why she broke a confidence.
    b) Think of all the other times she's let you down. You seek out someone else (who has also been let down by this friend) to talk about it and to confirm that your friend is a bitch.

17. You work in retail. You once thought it was what you wanted but it bores you. You now have the opportunity to apply for a job where you'll be more active.
    a) You jump at the chance and apply.

(Continued)

     b) You hesitate. You worry you are about to make another wrong choice.

18. Yesterday you stayed an hour late to complete a report. Your manager tells you she no longer needs the report for the meeting. You think:
    a) Damn! Oh well, some of what I wrote up will come in useful for another project or meeting.
    b) She must know how much time I spent writing this! I've done it all for nothing. What a complete waste of time. She's obviously decided to wind me up.

19. If you have friends over for a meal, you:
    a) Make a decent meal and enjoy having the company.
    b) Spend time on every aspect of the meal, candles, flowers etc. and get stressed about getting it all just right.

20. When you read your friends' social media posts it would appear that everyone is doing well in life. You think:
    a) Good for them!
    b) It just gets me down when I compare myself with them.

If you answered mostly a) – you are more of a positive thinker.

If you answered mostly b) – you are more of a negative thinker.

Look back at the answers. Notice how 'b)' answers all reflect the narrow thinking that contracts your world and limits your opportunities and possibilities. In contrast, 'a)' answers all reflect positive thinking that opens up possibilities and opportunities for you.

Cognitive distortions

Negative ways of thinking are often referred to as 'cognitive distortions'; illogical, irrational and unhelpful ways of thinking. Cognitive distortions are powerful because they can easily convince you that your thoughts *are* rational and true. But actually they are unhelpful; they misrepresent and limit your options. They can make you feel bad about the world, other people, yourself and your abilities.

Cognitive distortions are based on automatic thinking patterns that have been playing over and over in your mind, unchallenged, for years.

If you are predominantly a negative thinker, you may have a tendency to fall into particular patterns of cognitive distortions or negative thinking. Below are some examples.

Confirmation bias
Confirmation bias involves consciously or unconsciously looking for evidence to support and confirm what you've already decided is true, while avoiding or ignoring contradictory information.

You give too much weight to negative supporting information and opinions and too little to the positive elements of a situation.

For example, you tell a friend something personal and she tells another person. You feel betrayed. You then find yourself thinking back and noticing all sorts of 'wrong' behaviour from your friend that you have never given much thought to before. And then you seek out someone else (who doesn't like this friend) to talk about it and to confirm that your friend is a bitch. But you forget or ignore all the other ways in the past that your friend has been a good friend.

Another example would be if you tripped over and twisted your ankle and you thought, 'That'll teach me! I *knew* I shouldn't have sneaked off work today; I *thought* something would go wrong. It's my punishment.' Because you already feel you were wrong to sneak off work, you look for and accept evidence that you *have* done wrong. Rather than accept that you just weren't looking where you were going, you conclude that twisting your ankle just goes to confirm your wrongdoing.

Jumping to a conclusion
This involves judging or deciding something without having all the relevant information. You anticipate that things will turn out badly. For example, if, when someone lets you know that they need to speak with you about something, you immediately think 'It's something I've done wrong', then you jumped to a conclusion. Or if

you heard that redundancies were to be announced and you thought 'It's bound to be me. It's not fair', then you jumped to a conclusion. Instead of waiting until you have more information, you immediately react with a negative conclusion.

Tunnel thinking, polarized thinking and perfectionist thinking

Imagine looking down a cardboard tube. What can you see? Or rather, what can't you see? With tunnel thinking, you are blind to other possibilities and options. Instead of seeing the whole picture, you focus on the negative aspects. So if, for example, you are forced to change your holiday plans, and your thoughts are 'Why does this *always* happen to me? My plans are all ruined.' then you make it difficult to recognize that there are, in fact, other ways of thinking and doing things; you do have options.

Tunnel thinking is related to polarized thinking. It's 'all or nothing' thinking. With polarized thinking, there's no middle ground or grey areas. Things are black or white, good or bad, a success or a total failure, clever or stupid, there is no middle ground, no room for mistakes and no room for improvement.

These types of thoughts are often characterized by terms such as 'should' or 'shouldn't', 'must' or 'mustn't', 'every', 'always' or 'never'. For example, 'There's *absolutely no point* in voting. Things *never* change, *all* politicians are rubbish, and anyway, my vote won't make *any* difference.'

Also related to tunnel thinking and polarized thinking is perfectionist thinking. For example, if someone congratulates you on a piece of work you've done and you say; 'Thanks, but it wasn't that good,' and then tell them about the aspects that didn't go so well. In situations like this, for you, things have to be perfect or they don't count.

Catastrophizing

When you catastrophize, you work yourself up and think your way to disaster. You think the worst is going to happen in a situation. For example, if you have to drive somewhere new and you think 'I just know I'll get completely lost; I'll get confused and stressed; I won't know where I'm going; I won't know what to do,' then you're catastrophizing. That's fine if the worst case scenario prompts you to make plans to ensure the worst doesn't happen. But it's not helpful if anticipating the worst simply serves to overwhelm and paralyse you.

Mind reading

With mind reading, you believe you know what the other person is thinking and that their thoughts and intentions are negative. For example, if, when asked to work on an interesting project at work you thought: 'They only asked me because the other person couldn't do it. It wouldn't have occurred to them to ask me first', then you were mind reading. With this example, your negative thinking could undermine your confidence or make you feel resentful and so affect your ability to do well.

Blaming

This involves placing all responsibility for something that's gone wrong on someone or something else. If you see yourself as externally controlled, you see yourself as helpless, a victim of other people or external factors. If a group of people at work weren't working well together on a project and you thought 'This is never going to change – it's our manager's fault – he should've known this wouldn't work. Why did I have to be involved with this?' Blaming your manager for what's going wrong means that you feel (wrongly) that there's nothing you can do to put things right. You're at the mercy of others.

You might, though, place all the blame on yourself if things don't turn out well. Rightly or wrongly you may feel completely responsible for the well-being of others and the way events turn out. If things don't go well you feel guilty and blame yourself. That's fine if you are responsible and you do something to put things right, but it's not helpful if self-blame is misguided or it overwhelms you and prevents you from taking positive action.

Your explanatory style

Cognitive distortions and negative thinking patterns, then, narrow and reduce your options and opportunities and convince you that you have little or no control over your circumstances.

It's easy to assume that your negative thoughts are rational and true. But actually, they are limiting, unhelpful and even destructive. They can overwhelm you and trigger further unhelpful thoughts and reactions.

Because the way you think is habitual, you usually don't even recognize the nature of your thoughts and reactions to events. In fact, your thoughts are so powerful *because* you rarely have conscious awareness or control over them. Your mind simply accepts everything it's 'told' and you respond accordingly.

Many of your patterns of thinking and behaving will have developed over the years as a result of such things as your upbringing, family, friends, environment, education, media influences, religion and culture.

As we go about our daily life, our minds are continually thinking; interpreting and assessing our experiences, events and situations. But our brains have a limited ability to process everything that's going on. To make sense of what's going on, we've each developed an 'explanatory style'. This means that when something happens, has happened or is going to happen, your brain makes sense of it in a way that fits with your usual way of understanding events.

You have a system in your brain called the 'reticular activating system (RAS)' that controls your consciousness. The RAS filters out everything that doesn't support your most prevalent thoughts and behaviour. So, your mind has a tendency to, first and foremost, notice and pay attention to experiences that match its preexisting thoughts and beliefs.

If you're more inclined to think negatively, your brain will automatically interpret events in these negative ways. On the other hand, if you're more inclined to positive thinking, your brain will interpret and make sense of events in positive ways. And, whichever way you're inclined to think, each time you do, you reinforce that particular way of thinking, interpreting and explaining things.

Repeated negative ways of thinking can lead to a concept known as 'learned helplessness'.

This means that, in effect, you 'learn' or 'teach' yourself that you have little or no control over what happens to you, other people, situations and events.

Furthermore, having 'learned' to believe in your limitations and lack of control, you resign yourself to believing that more often than not, you are helpless and situations are often hopeless. Even if you become aware of your negative thinking, it can be a real struggle to think otherwise.

A constant stream of negative thoughts in your mind has prevented you from doing any creative problem-solving. The good news, though, is that your way of interpreting events does not have to be permanent and your outlook is not fixed. You *can* learn to think in a more positive, helpful way. You *can* overcome negative thinking by learning new, positive 'explanatory styles'.

Your amazing brain

It helps to further understand what's going on in your brain.

The core components of the brain are neurons; cells that process and transmit information. Neurons are connected to each other by neural pathways and networks.

So, when you think or do something new, a new neural pathway is created. Each time you think or behave in that particular way, your brain uses that same neural pathway. The pathway becomes stronger and stronger each time it's used. It's just like walking through a field of long grass – the more often that path is trodden, the more established the path becomes and the more likely it is that you'll take that path.

This is hugely beneficial to you because it means that if you do something often enough, it becomes automatic – you don't have to think about it. Think of the things you do on a daily basis that your brain and body are so used to that they don't even have to think about it – walking, talking, eating, brushing your teeth, driving, texting, etc.

However, this same process of neural pathways developing automatic ways of doing and thinking also establishes habits that are not so good for you: smoking, overeating, drinking, negative thinking and so on.

If you often interpret events in a negative way, then you create strong negative neural pathways in your brain.

Those neural pathways become so established that they also become habits; negative thinking habits that leave little or no room for more positive, helpful ways of thinking.

All is not lost! The good news is that if you change how you think or what you do, then new, positive neural pathways are formed. The RAS in your brain becomes more aware of and tuned in to positive events and possibilities. When you continue using these new positive pathways, they become stronger and deeper. Eventually, they will replace the old ways of thinking and behaving. You will have rewired – or reprogrammed – your brain.

Imagine, for example, that you need to learn to use your left hand instead of your right hand to write with a pen. It will take time and effort, because the neural pathway for using your right hand is well established. But if you really want to do it, you can forge new pathways and develop a new way of writing with a different hand.

The same is true for anything you want to do or any way you would like to think. Certainly it takes effort to change the way you think, but it is not impossible and it's never too late!

In a nutshell

- What you think and say to yourself can have quite an impact on what you can and can't do. Think positively and you'll feel able to manage. Think negatively and you're likely to feel overwhelmed and powerless.

- Emotions such as sadness, worry and guilt and their associated thoughts might not feel good yet they do have beneficial aspects: to prompt you to respond in helpful, positive ways.
- If you let 'negative' emotions and their negative thoughts overwhelm you, they can contract and distort your world and make you feel bad. Negative thoughts create a spiral of difficult thoughts and feelings.
- Cognitive distortions – such as confirmation bias, catastrophizing, mind reading and blaming – can easily convince you that your thoughts are rational and true. But actually, they are limiting and unhelpful.
- Because the way you think is habitual, you usually don't even recognize the nature of your thoughts and reactions to events. Your mind simply accepts everything it's 'told' and you respond accordingly.
- Whichever way you're inclined to think – positively or negatively – each time you do, you reinforce that particular way of thinking, interpreting and explaining things.
- Positive emotions and their associated positive thoughts open you up to new ideas and new experiences and possibilities. Positive thinking brings hope.
- You *can* overcome negative thinking by learning new 'explanatory styles': positive thinking.

2
Moving on from Negative Thinking

Recognize negative self-talk

Happiness doesn't depend on how few negative thoughts you have, but on what you do with the ones you have.

Lisa Esile

Because the way you think is habitual, you usually don't even recognize the nature of your thoughts and reactions to events. In fact, your negative thoughts are so powerful *because* you rarely have conscious awareness or control over them. You simply accept your thoughts and respond accordingly.

The first step, then, in managing negative thinking is simply to become more aware of it; to identify the way you think and to recognize your 'explanatory style'. Once you are more aware of your negative self-talk you can start to do something about it.

Chapter 1 will have given you an insight into the ways that you think. You can increase your awareness further by writing down some of your thoughts; thoughts about past, current or future events. Here are some ideas for how you could do that:

Past events

- Recall a couple of relatively unimportant events that were minor annoyances. For example, a travel delay, an event that got cancelled, something you lost. What thoughts went through your mind or could have been going through your mind? For example, if you missed the bus or train your thought may have been: 'Why does this always happen to me?' Write down what your thoughts and feelings were.
- Next think of bigger events – a job, a project at work, a holiday, a relationship or friendship where things didn't turn out well. What thoughts went through your mind or could have been going through your mind? How did you feel? Write it down.

Future events

- Think of an upcoming event that you're feeling unsure about; something you've got to do, somewhere you've got to go, someone you have to talk to, people you've got to meet. Whatever it is, what are your thoughts about it?
- Think of something good coming up; meeting up with friends, a holiday or a family celebration, for

example. What thoughts and feelings do you have about it? Are they mostly positive or negative? Again, write them down.

- Think of something you would like to do in future – travel somewhere, follow an interest or hobby, change your career direction, leave a job or relationship – but haven't done yet. Write down your thoughts and feelings about it.

Present events

- Over the course of the next few days, write down your thoughts and feelings about situations and events. Either write down your thoughts on paper (keep a pen and paper handy) text or email them to yourself, or make use of an app such as the Thought Diary Pro (an app designed to help people record unhelpful thoughts and beliefs). You won't be aware of every single thought, but when you do notice a negative thought, write it down. Don't pass any judgement on yourself for having this thought. Just be aware of it and write it down.
- Ask someone who you like and trust – a friend, partner, family member – to point out, over the next week or so, when they think you've made a negative comment. Write each one down.
- Use your feelings to alert you to how you are thinking: whenever you are feeling worried, stressed, annoyed or upset, stop and become aware of your thoughts. Write down your thoughts.

As well as being more aware of individual negative thoughts, you may notice a pattern or theme emerging.

You may realize that you're inclined to jump to conclusions or that you get caught up in tunnel thinking or catastrophizing. You may notice, too, what sort of events and experiences trigger your negative thoughts. Once you're more aware of your negative thoughts, you're in a better position to disempower them and to use them as a cue for positive action.

There are two approaches. The first approach involves challenging and replacing negative thinking. The second approach involves simply accepting negative thoughts and moving on to positive thoughts and actions.

Challenging and replacing negative thinking

Challenging negative thoughts can help you to see whether your view is reasonable and helpful. What you don't want to do, though, is to start arguing with yourself. Simply telling yourself you're 'wrong' to think the way you do won't work. You won't win! Your negative thoughts will probably win because they are so strongly established.

Instead, start by asking yourself 'Are these thoughts helping me?' Think about how your thinking is helping your situation.

For example, if, a few weeks before a driving test you think 'I'm going to fail my driving test. I'll be hopeless', the answer to the question 'Is this thought helping me?' could actually be 'Yes, it is helping me. It's making me realize I need to practise more.' But if an hour before the test, you think 'I'm going to fail my driving test. I'll be hopeless', then the thought is probably not helping you. Instead, it's overwhelming you and undermining your ability to think straight! It would be more helpful just to replace your negative thoughts with positive ones, such as, 'I've been taught well. I'll do the best I can.'

Let's take another example: imagine that yesterday you stayed at work an hour late to complete a report for your manager. This morning she tells you she doesn't need it for the meeting any more.

You think: 'She must know how much time I spent writing this up! I've done all that for nothing. Again. What a complete waste of time. She's obviously decided to wind me up.'

Ask yourself, 'In what way are these thoughts helpful?'

When you ask yourself 'Is this thought helpful?' you are not disputing the accuracy of your thoughts – maybe it *was* a waste of time, maybe she *is* trying to wind you up – but right now, regardless of their accuracy, these thoughts probably aren't helping you. They're preventing you from coming up with any solutions.

Are you certain?
The next step is to confront the certainty with which you feel your thoughts are absolutely right. Remember, if you are in the habit of negative thinking, it has become your default position – your mind automatically takes

and accepts a negative perspective without considering any other options.

So now you are challenging your mind's automatic negative perspective and recognize that there are other possibilities.

Here are some questions you could ask yourself:

- Am I positive that what I'm thinking is true?
- What evidence do I have for how I'm thinking about this situation?
- Do I know that for certain?
- Am I 100% sure?

Alternative perspectives

By challenging your automatic negative thoughts, by loosening your grip on what you are certain of, you free yourself to start thinking and responding in more positive ways.

Questions you could ask yourself next are:

- What is the evidence against the way I'm thinking about this situation/event?
- What other explanations are there for what happened, is happening or could happen?
- Is there anything positive and good about the situation?

In the example of the report that your manager no longer needed, it could be that the positive aspect of the situation was that you got more practice working on this kind of report. And, although your manager doesn't need the information now, it could be useful in future.

Recognizing that the way you're thinking doesn't make you feel good, or help you to get what you want, can prompt you to look at things from a different perspective.

So if, for example, you're forced to change your holiday plans and you think 'Why does this *always* happen to me? My plans are all ruined', ask yourself: 'In what way is this thought helpful? ('It's not helpful. It's just winding me up and making me feel sorry for myself.') 'Am I certain my plans are actually ruined?' ('Well no, they're not completely ruined. I'll think of an alternative place to go.') 'Is there anything positive about the situation?' ('Yes. I still have a week off work and my friend is still able to go with me.')

As well as loosening your grip on what you think you're certain of, challenging your negative thoughts not only interrupts your thoughts but it also stops them from snowballing.

Replacing negative thinking with positive thinking
When you're in the habit of thinking and interpreting events in a negative way, it's not easy to say positive things to yourself. It's also not easy to say positive things to yourself when you're worried, stressed or upset. It's not easy but it *is* possible.

A few years ago, shortly after leaving university, Sam was offered a position in business administration at a large company in Manchester.

I used to get into a right state about attending meetings at my new job. I thought that everyone else was more knowledgeable and more articulate than me. I dreaded being put on the spot and being asked a question that I might not know the answer to.

What changed things was some advice from a lovely, understanding colleague – Erik – who I confided in. He wasn't a counsellor but I now realize the questions he asked me sort of 'coached' me through my negative thinking patterns and helped me to think differently. He asked me, prior to a meeting, what exactly my thoughts were about it. We talked about where I was catastrophizing or mind reading and how helpful or unhelpful it was for me to think in these ways.

It became quite amusing coming up together with alternative, more positive ways of thinking about the meetings. Basically, Erik helped me to focus on the positive – to recognize that I was much more of a listener than a talker – that my strength was my ability to easily make sense of what some people waffled on about and clarify that for myself and others in the meetings.

Erik gave me a top tip too – he suggested that if he wasn't around, whenever I lapsed into negative thinking, I should get up and change my surroundings. He said 'Sam, just go for a walk – even if only to the other side of the room. Let the change in your surroundings prompt change in your thinking.'

That was ten years ago, I'm fine about meetings now but I still use Erik's 'go for a walk' tip. It still works!

Turn back to the questionnaire in Chapter 1. Look at how each situation contained a negative response *and* an alternative, positive response.

Now read over any negative thoughts you wrote down in response to past, present and future situations at the beginning of this chapter. What other, more positive thoughts *might* have been possible instead? Look at each one and come up with some ideas for more positive thoughts to replace the negative thoughts.

If you find this hard, it might be because you can't imagine yourself thinking in a different way. Try taking a step back and depersonalizing the process; think of yourself as a script writer – imagine you are simply writing alternative thoughts and lines for a character in a play. With the alternative, more positive thoughts, be sure to keep them plausible and realistic enough for you to believe them.

For example, if you think 'I'm hopeless. I've made another mistake. Everyone must think I'm stupid', there's no need to change it to 'I'm brilliant! I do everything really well. Everyone must think I'm amazing.' That's just another cognitive distortion; an overly positive one! Instead, replace it with something like 'I try my best. Sometimes I make mistakes but I can learn from them. Nobody is expecting me to be perfect.'

Do make the new positive thought something that *feels* believable to you, otherwise your mind will not accept it as a real possibility.

Cognitive Behavioural Therapy

This way of challenging your negative thinking and replacing it with positive thoughts is based on Cognitive Behavioural Therapy (CBT) – an approach that can help you change the way you think and, therefore, the way you behave.

CBT suggests that whichever way you interpret a situation you will respond accordingly. If you change the way you think, you will create a change in how you feel, what you do and how you behave. So, for example, rather than think 'My holiday plans are ruined', you might think 'My plans are not ruined, I *can* change my plans.' Thinking in this way makes you feel more hopeful and better able to respond in a positive, helpful way.

With CBT you identify, challenge and replace unhelpful, negative thoughts. This enables you to change your behaviour in future.

Anything and everything, then, can be explained in a positive or negative way. The trick is to choose the most positive and plausible interpretation and to tell that to yourself. Doing this can then positively influence how you respond to situations.

Accepting negative thoughts and moving on to positive thoughts and actions

CBT techniques – challenging and replacing negative thoughts – have been found to be very effective in helping people to change the way they think and behave.

Recently, another approach has emerged – an approach that is based on mindfulness. It's known as Acceptance and Commitment Therapy (ACT). Acceptance and Commitment Therapy suggests that you don't start by directly challenging negative thinking. You still need to be aware of negative thoughts and recognize when they are unhelpful, but you don't spend time and effort on challenging them.

Instead, an acceptance and commitment approach encourages you to acknowledge and accept your negative thoughts and just step back from them. You then commit yourself to more positive thoughts, actions and behaviour that correspond with what you want from a situation. The focus is on what you can positively do about your situation, rather than on trying to challenge, question and analyse your thoughts.

There are three steps: acceptance, diffusion and committing.

1. Acceptance

With an acceptance and commitment approach, it's recognized that trying to suppress or deny negative thoughts can take up a lot of unnecessary energy; energy that could be used in more helpful, positive ways.

So, you start by acknowledging and accepting your thoughts about a situation and you accept what is beyond your control.

For example, with the thoughts: 'She must know how much time I spent writing this! I've done it all for nothing. Again. What a complete waste of time. She's obviously decided to wind me up', you simply acknowledge those thoughts and accept them. You accept that they're negative and that they're not helping you.

2. Diffusion

When you become caught up in negative thinking, you become what ACT calls being 'fused' with your thoughts. It's as though you and your thoughts have melded together and become one.

For example: think to yourself 'I am an orange.' When you did this you may have then thought 'I'm an orange ... er ... right ... OK then ...' It's a thought you had, but you didn't automatically believe it. (Did you?)

However, when you have thoughts like 'I'm hopeless' you 'fuse' with those thoughts; you let them define who and what you are. But you don't have to let them define you or your reality. Especially as they're not helpful! Diffusion involves separating yourself from negative thoughts. Instead of getting caught up, struggling or getting fused with your thoughts, you notice them and let them go.

Imagine, for example, a sheriff in an old Western town who notices an outlaw strolling down the main street. The sheriff acknowledges the outlaw and then calmly and firmly encourages him to keep walking, right on out of town. That's you, acknowledging those negative thoughts and then calmly telling them to keep moving along out of your mind. Instead of challenging your negative thoughts, you simply acknowledge and release them. If and when they come back, look them in the eye like that sheriff and tell them what they need to do – keep moving along.

With diffusion, you experience your thoughts as nothing more than an ever-changing stream of words, sounds and pictures. You don't analyse them or dwell on them and you don't challenge them by asking, for example, 'Am I sure that what I'm thinking is true?' and 'What evidence do I have for how I'm thinking about this situation?' Instead, you notice the negative thoughts and let them go so you can move on to more helpful ways of thinking, responding and behaving.

Just realizing that your mind is thinking negative thoughts means you have already begun to de-fuse from those thoughts; separated yourself a little bit from them. Writing them down can separate you from them too – instead of letting negative thoughts swirl around in your mind, you can see your thoughts as just letters and words on paper.

3. Commitment

When negativity overwhelms you, the emotional (limbic) part of your brain takes over and the thinking part of your brain (neocortex) shuts down.

When you accept and let go of negative thoughts and feelings, you give the neocortex – the rational, logical part of your mind – the opportunity to start working for you; to think in more helpful, positive ways. You can think about what is important to you in a situation, plan and take action accordingly.

For example, with the thoughts: 'She must know how much time I spent writing this! I've done it all for nothing. Again. What a complete waste of time. She's obviously decided to wind me up.' You simply acknowledge and accept that it's not helping you to stay stuck in those thoughts and you move on to thinking what positive thoughts or action you can take.

And if, for example, you have the opportunity for a career change, instead of thinking 'I'd have to retrain, the money wouldn't be as good for the first couple of years, I'd need to re-organize childcare ...' you accept but then let go of those doubtful, negative thoughts. You then commit yourself, your time and energy to finding positive solutions to retraining, finances, childcare etc.

An acceptance and commitment approach emphasizes that no matter what you thought before, what matters now is how you think from now on. In fact, just thinking about what you have to gain rather than what you have to lose will help you let go of negativity.

'Turn your face to the sun and the shadows fall behind you.'

Maori proverb

In a nutshell

- Once you're more aware of your negative thoughts, you're in a better position to disempower them and to use them as a cue for positive action.
- Challenging the way you're thinking, and recognizing that it doesn't make you feel good or help you to get what you want, can prompt you to look at things from a different perspective.
- When you replace negative thoughts, you're looking to see what positive thoughts might be possible instead.
- Be sure to phrase your alternative, positive thoughts in terms that are plausible and realistic enough for you to believe them.
- Anything and everything can be explained in a positive or negative way. A Cognitive Behavioural Therapy (CBT) approach suggests that you choose the most helpful, positive and plausible interpretation and tell that to yourself. Doing this can then positively influence how you respond to situations.

- An 'acceptance and commitment' approach encourages you simply to accept and then let go of negative thoughts and instead commit yourself, your time and energy to positive thoughts and solutions.

3
Taking Positive Action

Can positive thinking really get you what you want in life?

Back in 2006 a best-selling book, *The Secret*, was published. It suggests that if you clearly and specifically visualize what you want, it can be yours.

The Secret is based on the 'law of attraction'. The law of attraction claims that every positive or negative event that happens to you is 'attracted' by you and your thoughts. Want to run a successful business or work in a job you love? With positive thinking you can attract that. Want a top of the range BMW? You can attract that too simply by (and here's the secret) sending positive thoughts out to the universe. You send a request to the universe which is, apparently, created by thoughts and therefore responds to thoughts.

Something gone wrong in your life? Someone behaved unfairly to you? Well, with negative thinking you will have attracted that as well. That's because the law of attraction brings to each person the conditions and experiences that they predominantly think about or expect.

The Secret has three basic steps: ask, believe and receive. Ask the universe for it. Identify something you want or need in your life and then simply place the order with the cosmos by asking for it. The universe will answer. Think positively and see what you want as *already* yours. You'll need to know exactly what it is that you want. If you're not clear, the universe will get an unclear frequency and will send you unwanted results.

The truth – or the real secret – is that the 'law of attraction' (also known as 'cosmic ordering') is based on a concept better known as confirmation bias. Confirmation bias (as described in Chapter 1) involves looking for evidence and information to support and confirm what you've already decided is true, while avoiding or ignoring information that contradicts it.

If you tripped over and twisted your ankle, the law of attraction would claim that you had 'attracted' that to happen to you as a result of your negative thinking. By thinking 'That'll teach me! I knew I shouldn't have sneaked off work today; I knew something would go wrong. It's my punishment', you looked for and accepted evidence that you had done wrong.

If you found a parking space in a packed car park, the law of attraction would claim that you had 'attracted' that parking space from the universe and as a result of your positive expectation that a space would be there, waiting for you.

The Secret and the law of attraction exploit the concept of confirmation bias and suggest that the positive and negative things that happen in our lives are the result of a mystical force. It exploits the fact that our brains naturally choose what we pay attention to. The law of attraction suggests your mind attracts thoughts and experiences as a result of the workings of the universe. *It doesn't.* Your mind attracts these thoughts and experiences as a result of the workings of your *brain.*

In Chapter 1 you will have read how, for the sake of speed and ease, your mind notices and pays attention to experiences that match its preexisting thoughts and beliefs. So, if you already feel you've done wrong and you trip and twist your ankle, your brain (not the universe) is predisposed to being aware of any negative events that you experience. And if you were looking hopefully for a parking space, your brain and all your senses (not the universe) were already on high alert to notice a space. The parking space didn't just appear; you were actively looking for it.

There's no mystery – and there's no secret. The law of attraction and cosmic ordering are simply mystic terms for goal setting and positive confirmation bias.

Positive thinking and positive action

Whatever way you choose to see it, positive thinking alone won't get you what you want. Positive thinking will not 'attract' positive events from the universe. You can't just think about it and hope to attract it! You actually have to follow up your positive thinking by *doing* something. Doing something positive. You must take action to run a successful business or work in a job you love or afford a top of the range BMW.

Whatever it is you want, you must plan, put in time and effort and work towards achieving what you want. You have to make the most of opportunities, take some risks and be prepared to deal with obstacles, setbacks and disappointments.

Positive thinking can't replace positive action. What positive thinking *does* do is encourage proactive behaviour, and pragmatic ways to accomplish goals, overcome obstacles and manage setbacks. If you combine positive thinking with positive action, you'll be more likely to get positive results.

How to get what you want and achieve your goals

'Success depends on your backbone not your wishbone.'
Kamari aka Lyrikal

Having things that you want to do and achieve – having goals and aims – can give you a positive path to follow. In fact, working towards goals both requires and develops optimism and positivity.

Write down something you'd like to do; something you'd like to achieve. It could be a short-term goal; something you want to achieve in the next few days or weeks, or a longer-term goal; something you want to achieve in the next few months or years in your life.

Maybe it's to do with your health; you might want to lose weight, stop smoking, take up running, be able to walk up a hill without being out of breath.

It could be something you'd like to learn or improve; playing a musical instrument or learning a language, for example.

Maybe it's something to do with work – change career, work freelance or run your own business, do some voluntary work, work abroad, return to study.

Perhaps you want to travel; visit New York, Cuba, Asia, Australia or New Zealand.

It could be that you have a problem to be solved; you want a cleaner, tidier home, to manage a difficult person, leave a job, a university course or a relationship.

Or maybe you want to write a book, join a band or a choir, win a talent show, feel more confident, make new friends, do something creative, grow your own vegetables, decorate a room in your home or sort out a box of family photos.

If you have something specific you want to do – a clear goal such as to write and complete a novel in the next two years, or to run a marathon next April, then fine. But if it's more general – to travel, to be happier, healthier, to get on better with your sister, then for the moment, that's OK too. (The next step – identifying your options – will help you identify how, specifically, you could achieve your wider goal.)

If your goal is an issue or problem that you want to deal with, think about what the result or outcome will be once the problem has been solved. What do you see yourself doing? For example, if the problem is university and you want to leave, then, for you, the outcome of leaving university might be that you will be working to save up to go travelling. Or, if you want to get on better with your sister, what will you both be able to do that would confirm that things have improved between you?

State your goal as a positive statement
To increase your chances of achieving any goal, think of a positive goal with a positive outcome. Goals that are framed in such terms as 'mustn't', 'can't' or 'won't', 'shouldn't' or 'stop', 'lose' or 'quit' are unlikely to motivate you.

Instead of thinking, for example, 'I must stop eating junk' think 'I want to eat more healthily'. And instead of thinking 'I hate this job and everyone who works here. I want to leave' think 'I want to go to a job that I enjoy where I like the people I work with'. Thinking like this creates positive energy and momentum instead of feelings of deprivation and resentment.

Goals framed in positive terms tell you what to do rather than what not to do. You are more likely to achieve goals that get you what you want, rather than goals that tell you to avoid something.

Go back to your reasons for doing what you want to do. Are you sure they are framed in positive terms? If not, rewrite them.

Write down your options

Now, write down your options; all the possible ways you could get what you want and achieve your goal. However big or small your ideas about the different ways you could achieve something, write them down.

If you keep your ideas and options in your head, it's difficult to tap into more expansive thinking. There's only a certain amount of information your brain can hold before that information just clutters your mind. Writing your thoughts and ideas down not only empties your brain, it can also bring out more ideas.

Ideas can be realistic or unrealistic; it doesn't matter because the important thing at this stage is simply to imagine all sorts of possibilities. Ask yourself, for example, what you would do if there was nothing to stop you – you didn't have to think about money or other people. Think, too, about what has and hasn't worked in the past in relation to what it is you want to achieve.

If, for example, your long-term goal is that a year from now you'll have bounced back from redundancy and be happy and successful, then imagine all the ways that could happen. There may be several options. For example, you could look for similar employment in your area or move areas; perhaps you could work freelance, work abroad or change career direction. And if you wanted to learn to play the ukulele, you might identify four options: to find a local class, to hire a tutor, to learn through online tuition or to swap a skill you have in return for ukulele tuition.

The process of identifying your options will stretch you beyond your usual way of thinking and behaving. And because positive thinking broadens and opens up possibilities and ideas, you may find that some of your ideas spark other ideas.

Remember: write your ideas down, so that you can actually see them. Don't let your ideas stay stuck in your head. Once you've got some ideas and options written down, for each option, ask yourself some questions:

- What skills, strengths and resources do you currently have that could be helpful for each option?
- What further research and information do you need?
- Who could help?

- Who could give you advice and ideas?
- What resources might you need?
- When do you expect the goal to be achieved by?
- When could you get started? (Depending on your goal, it could take time to get all the information you need to make an informed choice.)

Now think about the 'pros' and 'cons' of each option. Write them down. Be aware of how a particular option or idea makes you feel right now, when you think about it. If you feel positive and inspired, and feel it's a realistic, achievable way forward, then it's the right option. It becomes your specific goal.

Knowing you have options gives you the power of choice; you get to decide what way forward would work best for you.

Take a step-by-step approach

'How do you eat an elephant? One bite at a time.'

Whatever it is you want to do and whichever option you choose, although it may present a challenge, it shouldn't be too hard or difficult.

It can be daunting and disheartening to think how much time and effort you've got to put in – for example, if you know you've only got two months to learn to play the ukulele at your brother's wedding in August. Or that you want to lose a stone in weight by Christmas.

So, what needs to happen is for a goal to be broken down into smaller, more doable steps. Taking a step-by-step approach is the most positive way forward because it means you set yourself up for constant successes by achieving small targets along the way.

So now, write down all the things you think you'd need to do towards your goal. Just empty your mind; you don't need to write things down in any particular order just yet.

If, for example, you wanted to change career direction, the things you'd need to do could include talking to a careers advisor or coach, spending time online researching jobs and training in the career you're interested in and rewriting your CV. These are all part of the larger goal, but breaking them down makes them easier to think about and to work on.

Next, plan the tasks – the steps you need to take – and think through how and when you'll do them. Make a written list, outlining your steps. It's easier to get straight on to the next step if you have already planned what to do and how you are going to do it. It allows you to maintain a steady pace and keep the pace going.

Ask yourself:

- What are you going to do first?
- When, exactly?
- What will be the next step after that?

Tell yourself 'This is what I'm going to do next' and have just one thing you can do right now. What's the first step you can take? What will be the next? Each time you achieve a small part of your goal, you get a sense of achievement, and see yourself getting closer to getting what you want.

Often, all that's needed to gain the momentum to tackle the whole project is to complete the first step. And then move on to the next step. And then the next one. Each step may or may not be challenging in some way. If it feels overwhelming or too difficult, break that step down into a few smaller steps.

Even with the steps that you find challenging, you can recognize that every task you complete brings you closer to the ultimate goal. For example, when I'm decorating a room, as much as I dislike sanding down woodwork, I keep in mind that once I've completed the sanding, I'm one step closer to the room being completely decorated. And that's positive thinking!

What could feel impossible in one giant leap becomes a lot more doable as a series of smaller steps. There's nothing new about this process – it's something you've done many times before. Any task, activity or goal, anything you've achieved – from getting up and going to work, to organizing a party to moving house – has been as a result of a series of steps.

Doing things one step at a time also gives you time to look at what is working and what isn't, and to decide if you need to change tactics. So, as you go through each step, review the outcome. What's worked? What helped and went well?

Identifying goals and options and taking it one step at a time is the approach that helped Leo Babauta to get out of debt. In his blog zenhabits.net Leo explains that it all started in 2005 with his goal to quit smoking, a goal Leo attributes to setting a chain of other positive changes in motion. In his blog, Leo writes: 'Quitting smoking taught me a lot about changing habits and accomplishing goals, and all the elements needed to make this successful. I had tried and failed to quit smoking before, and when I was successful this time, I analysed it and learned from it and was inspired by my success. Success can breed success, if you take advantage of it.'

Leo says that in order to relieve stress without smoking, he took up running. He started out by running about half a mile and slowly built up his distance and within a month was running his first 5K. Very soon, he was so into running that he decided to run his first marathon.

'In order to get my running in, I decided to start waking early. Once I began waking early, I began to discover the joys of the quiet morning hours. I get so much more done in the morning – not work, but working on my goals.'

Leo was able to rid himself of his debts in a little over two years while supporting his wife and family of six children. 'I stopped living paycheck-to-paycheck and learned how to stick to my budget, spend less, save and pay off debts. I started with some smaller bills in 2006, and paid off every single debt by the end of 2007. It was amazing! I now live debt-free.'

Leo's been debt-free since that time and has gone on to create one of the most popular blogs on the planet in Zen Habits. You can read more about how he did this at www.zenhabits.net/my-story/.

A warning about deadlines
Knowing when you want to achieve something by helps focus your efforts on completing and achieving what you want to do. Be careful, though, not to become overly concerned with deadlines.

You may be someone who is motivated by reaching deadlines and achieving targets. Great! On the other hand, you might be someone who is more 'process orientated'. This means that, for you, saying, for example, 'I want to lose a stone by Christmas' or 'I want to have changed my job by April' isn't always the best mindset.

Although pressure can be positive and motivating, it can also create stress. If you don't meet the deadline or reach your target, you risk feeling like you failed (even if you are better off than you were at the start). Or you might be concerned about the time it is going to take to achieve what you want; you worry that if, for example, you start working freelance now, it could take months to build up enough clients to make it worthwhile. Or that if you leave your partner, it might be a long time before you meet someone else.

Instead of giving yourself a deadline to reach or thinking about how long it will take, know that a step-by-step plan allows you simply to work consistently towards what it is you want to achieve, however long it takes.

'No matter how many mistakes you make or how slow you progress, you're still way ahead of anyone who isn't trying.'

Tony Robbins

Of course, some goals have an inherent deadline – if you want to learn to dance the tango for your wedding on August 12th, you can't really change that date. What you can do, though, is give yourself a flexible plan to follow – increasing the amount of practice you need to do – rather than have the pressure of a deadline looming towards you.

Remember – you're aiming to think positively. Tell yourself 'I have a plan. I can manage this.' Just know to focus on one thing at a time.

Positive visualizing

Often, when you are going to do something, you visualize it first. It's a natural process. If, for example, you think about a trip to another country you have to make, you might visualize going from your home to the station or bus stop. Then you visualize the train journey to the airport, then the time you'll spend at the airport and then the flight. You then visualize arriving at your destination and making your way to the car hire place.

You then visualize getting to the city or place that is your final destination.

This process of imagining is useful to help you do just about anything you want to do and 'see' the steps or key elements to make it happen.

When you imagine yourself doing something, your brain creates the neural pathways that you will use when it comes to doing something for real. Visualizing is like someone going ahead and beating a path for you through the jungle – they've prepared the way ready for when you come along in that direction; the path has been made easier for you.

Furthermore, this process of visualizing programs your brain to be aware of and recognize resources and information, ideas and opportunities that could help you to achieve your goals. It's positive confirmation bias; it raises your awareness of positive possibilities.

So, if you had visualized travelling to a particular area in France and someone at work mentioned restaurants in that part of France, your ears would prick up; you'd be more alert to that information. It's your brain's reticular activating system working for you; bringing to your attention relevant information.

Furthermore, if you can imagine yourself achieving something, your brain then believes and accepts that it *is*, indeed, possible and that you *can* do it. The future you see is the future you get. (If you constantly visualize *not* being able to do something, your brain believes and accepts that too.) Your brain can't tell the difference between having visualized making that journey to a foreign country, for example, and having done it for real.

And, as you know, if you've done something successfully once, you're more likely to believe you can do it again. This helps build confidence. And that's positive thinking!

Be flexible

Whatever you want to do and however you've chosen to go about it, you don't need to have fixed plans. As you work towards whatever it is that you want to achieve, you may need to adjust the steps you intend to take as a result of new knowledge and experience.

You will need to be flexible and open to the fact that problems might arise. Be prepared to change course in light of the unexpected. This doesn't mean that you're giving up on a great idea. It means that you're not limiting your chance of success by focusing on just one way to accomplish it.

If, when you were planning how to achieve your goal, you looked at all your options for achieving what you wanted, you would already have identified a Plan B.

It can be helpful to have a Plan B; an option that you can implement if the original one proves impractical or unsuccessful. Whether it's a journey, a change of career or getting fitter or improving a relationship with a friend or family member, things happen. The weather changes, someone doesn't want to take part, health problems come up, it costs more money than you expected. But, if you really want to get what you want, there is always a way. And, most likely, there's more than one way!

In a nutshell

- You attract particular thoughts and experiences not as a result of the workings of the universe, but as a result of the workings of your *brain*.
- Having things that you want to do and achieve – having goals and aims – can give you a positive path to follow, but you do have to follow up your positive thinking by *doing* something, taking positive action.
- Knowing you have options gives you the power of choice; you get to decide what way forward would work best for you.
- Taking a step-by-step approach is the most positive way forward because it means you set yourself up for constant successes by achieving small targets along the way. And see yourself getting closer to getting what you want.
- It's easier to get straight on to the next step if you have already planned what to do and how you are going to do it. It allows you to maintain a steady pace and keep the pace going. It also gives you time to look at what is working and what isn't, and to decide if you need to change tactics.

- Instead of giving yourself a deadline to reach, simply focus on working consistently towards what it is you want to achieve, one step at a time.
- Visualizing creates the neural pathways that you will use when it comes to doing something for real. Visualizing also programs your brain to be aware of resources and information, ideas and opportunities that could help you to achieve your goals.
- Be prepared to change course in light of the unexpected. This does not mean that you are giving up on a great idea. It means that you're not limiting your chance of success by focusing on just one way to accomplish it.

PART 2

Developing and Maintaining Positive Thinking

4
Finding and Keeping Motivation

You've probably heard a joke where the punchline is 'The light bulb has to want to change.' But whatever it is you want to do, whatever goals you're aiming to achieve, it's quite possible that despite your good intentions, you can't get yourself started or you can't keep motivated.

Maybe you haven't put money aside for savings (you've seen something you want to buy first). Perhaps you didn't make a start on all that paperwork last night (there was something good to watch on TV). And you're certainly not going to go for a run today; it's cold outside!

Perhaps there's something you want to do but you're waiting for something or someone in your life to change before you take positive action. Maybe you think you need to be more knowledgeable and confident, prepared or secure to move forward with what you want to achieve or do.

You may hear yourself say some of the following:

- I'm not ready
- It's not the right time
- It's going to be too hard
- It will take too long
- Maybe I'm not meant to do it
- I'm too old/too young
- It's too late
- I don't have enough money/time/experience
- I don't have the energy or the commitment
- I'm scared
- I might not do it right
- People will laugh at me
- Most people don't succeed, so neither will I
- I'm not good enough
- I'll start tomorrow/next week/next year.

These excuses can often sound quite convincing. But if you believe them, if you stay in your comfort zone, doing the same old activities and tasks on autopilot and not trying anything new, you could well be missing out. Nothing will change and you won't get what you want in life.

Whatever you want to do or achieve, there will always be a new problem standing in your way, or something you need to do before you can fully commit yourself. You can sit around and plan, waiting for everything to be just right, but nothing is ever going to happen until you actually start getting on with it.

So how to get motivated and stay motivated? By thinking positively, of course!

First of all, keep in mind the good reasons. You must have a reason to achieve what it is you want. Why is it so important to you? What will be the benefits of achieving what it is you want? Maybe it's a financial or material gain. Perhaps it's personal gain; you'll be happier or wiser, or you will learn something new, be healthier or improve yourself or your situation in some way. Whatever it is, keep it in mind. Even better, write it down and pin it up where you can see it every day as a regular reminder.

Acting 'as if'

'To change one's life, start immediately. Do it flamboyantly. No exceptions.'

William James

Don't expect to magically 'feel like it' before taking action. Instead, expect that it's normal *not* to feel like it in the beginning. But instead of using energy to avoid getting going, be prepared to move through that reluctant feeling on your way to achieving what you want. That's what successful people do. They often don't feel like getting started either.

Cara is a freelance writer:

It starts with me having a good idea for an article. I email my idea to a number of magazine editors and when one of them commissions me to write the article, I'm thrilled. But then I actually have to write it! Most mornings, I don't feel like writing. At least, not initially. What makes me do it? It's not because I have amazing willpower, it's because I know that 'feeling like it' rarely comes before taking action.

But I've learnt that pretty much every time, I sit down with my laptop and even though I don't feel like it initially, I start writing, and before I know it, I'm absorbed in writing.

So that's what gets me started – knowing that I will feel like it if I just get started.

If you're waiting until you feel completely confident and certain about something before you take action, or you've made a start and now you've stalled, you may find that acting 'as if' will help. Acting 'as if' is a way to create motivation to do something even though you may not feel like doing it.

Though it might feel artificial and forced in the beginning, get started on whatever it is you hope to achieve and quite soon the momentum takes over and you find yourself easily carrying on with whatever it is you intended to do. All it takes is a little effort at the start.

Five minutes of positive action

Whatever it is that you need to make a start on, make a deal with yourself: tell yourself you'll do it for just five minutes. Answer one email. Run one time around the block.

Instead of putting things off – instead of trying to clean the entire kitchen, for example, or arrange every aspect of a holiday or answer all those emails or sort through all those photos – tell yourself you'll do it for just five minutes. Start doing something immediately, without thinking and giving your mind time to come up with excuses. Start on what you intend to do immediately, before you begin to doubt your abilities or fear that you'll fail.

You may well find that, once you get going, you end up continuing well past the five-minute mark you'd decided on. If even the smallest task seems too hard, tell yourself you're just going to do five minutes right now. Make it ridiculously easy. Make it easy for yourself to get started on the things you do actually want to achieve.

The five-minute rule works for any goal for one simple reason: the physics of real life. As Sir Isaac Newton discovered, objects at rest tend to stay at rest, but objects in motion tend to stay in motion. This is just as true for humans as it is for falling apples! When you act 'as if', you generate the physical motions, which, in turn, can trigger the thoughts – the positive thoughts – which correspond to that physical action.

Once you start doing something, it's easier to continue doing it. Take action and things will flow from there. That's why it's important to have a plan for the steps

(Continued)

you need to take; it's easier if you know what you're doing first and what step comes next.

Decide what is the one thing you can do right now. Then do that one thing. Give it your full attention. Answer that one email, make that first phone call. Start filling in that form. Just clear out one drawer. Put just one thing on eBay. Paint one wall. Sign up for that class. Write the first paragraph. Book the flight. Arrange to meet. Sign up to that internet dating site. Get your running shoes on and get out the door! All sorts of good things can happen once you get started.

After a short time, the positive feelings which you would like to achieve from doing that activity start to emerge naturally. You don't have to wait for your thoughts and feelings to change before you get going. Get going and your feelings will change.

Once you understand and accept the logic, it's easier to change your mindset and focus on the positive; that is, what you'll regularly achieve even with the smallest activities for even the shortest time.

Need to have a difficult conversation with someone? Write down your opening lines, read them out loud to yourself and then jump right in. The conversation will go on from there – it may go well or it may not, but at least you've opened up communication.

Nervous about going to a meeting or party? Behave in a more outgoing, interested and friendly way for the first five minutes even if you don't feel like it. Initially it will feel forced and unnatural, but other people will respond to you as if you are quite naturally outgoing, interested and friendly.

It's a positive feedback loop – acting 'as if' positively influences further thoughts and actions. Don't wait for your feelings to change to take the action. Just take the action and see how your thoughts and feelings change.

Now, what's the first step you can take to make it easier for you to get started on the things you do actually want to achieve? You have the power. Plug it in.

Make it even easier

Whatever it is you want to do, spend a minute or two setting it up so that it's easier to go forward than to do nothing. Want to go for a swim or a run each morning but can't get your act together? Put your swimming costume or running gear on before you get properly dressed. That way you're far more likely to make a start. Try it, with no expectation other than to see what it's like.

Change your body, change your mind

'Our bodies change our minds, and our minds can change our behaviour, and our behaviour can change our outcomes.'

Amy Cuddy

Motivation is made up of three aspects – what you think, what you feel and what you do. Positively adopt just one of those aspects and you will positively affect the other two aspects. This is why the 'as if' principle is so effective; you positively change what you do and before you know it, how you think and feel has changed too.

People in particular professions often use the act 'as if' principle when they have to deal with difficult, challenging situations. For example, medical staff, police officers, social workers, rescue workers etc. will behave in a calm, confident way in unpredictable or potentially dangerous situations; they act 'as if' – as if they are calm and confident right from the start and the feelings follow through.

Recent research suggests that the way you sit or stand can actually affect the way your brain functions. Carry yourself with confidence and in a matter of minutes, the chemical balance – the testosterone and cortisol levels in the brain – alters, your body starts to feel it and your brain starts to believe it.

Dana Carney, an assistant professor at Columbia Business School, led a study where she split volunteers into two groups. The people in one group were asked to sit or stand in 'power poses'. Some were seated at desks, asked to put their feet up on the table, look straight ahead and interlock their hands behind the back of their heads. Others stood straight, feet apart, head up and hands on hips. Another group of people were asked to sit or stand in closed postures; curled and hunched and looking at the ground.

The researchers then took blood samples from the volunteers. Those people whose poses were open had significantly higher levels of testosterone – the hormone associated with feelings of power – and lower levels of cortisol – the stress hormone.

The volunteers were asked how they felt, too. In contrast to the volunteers who had adopted closed poses, those who had adopted the open, expansive postures felt more confident and positive.

So, how you sit or stand can change how you think or feel. In fact, if you adopt just a couple of positive body language poses or gestures, you can make a big difference to how you think and feel.

In her fascinating TED Talk (www.ted.com/speakers/amy_cuddy), Harvard social psychologist Amy Cuddy explains how, by focusing on just one or two aspects of your body language, you can directly influence the message your brain will receive.

You don't have to learn a whole new repertoire of poses, gestures and expressions that feel unnatural or uncomfortable. If you can hold just a couple of poses or gestures consistently, the rest of your body and mind will catch up and you will *feel* more confident and *come across* as more confident and capable.

Read through this list of actions and choose two that would be most comfortable for you to adopt when you want to feel more positive and confident:

- stand or sit straight
- keep your head level
- relax your shoulders
- spread your weight evenly on both legs
- if sitting, keep your elbows on the arms of your chair (rather than tightly against your sides)
- make appropriate eye contact
- lower the pitch of your voice
- speak more slowly.

You can't control *all* your nonverbal communication; in fact, the harder you try, the more unnatural you're likely to feel. But if you can keep your mind on doing one or two of those things consistently, your thoughts, feelings and behaviour can match up. Which one or two actions would you feel comfortable using? You can practise using them right now.

Where there's a will there's a way!

So where does willpower – the ability to do what you intend to do when you don't feel like doing it – fit in?

Maybe you've got started on what it is you want to achieve but worry that you won't have the willpower or self-control to keep going and achieve what you want.

You may, for example, want to improve your health – maybe you're trying to quit smoking or drink less, eat more healthily or take more exercise. Despite your intentions, you've lapsed back into your old ways.

Perhaps you've made a start on your novel but you just can't find the resolve to keep going. You're determined to make some headway today but you sit down and get lost in social media or another distraction instead.

You *can* do something about it; you can develop your willpower.

Willpower can provide the kickstart you need to get going and keep going. It gives you an inner determination that drives you forward. Together with self-control, willpower gives you the ability to keep focused and achieve your goals through self-discipline. Willpower helps you do what's best for you.

But if it helps you do what's best for you, why is willpower so difficult? Because, according to many studies, we all have a limited amount of willpower and it is easily used up. In any one day, you can be faced with countless little decisions: what to wear, what to eat, where to eat, where to go, how to get there, what time to come and go, who to talk to, who not to talk to, who to email, what to watch, what to listen to and so on. Individually, most of these decisions are fairly straightforward. But all together, in any one day, they add up exponentially – at a steady and often rapid rate.

Research shows that willpower is actually rather like a kind of muscle; it can get tired if you overuse it. In a number of studies, Florida State University's Dr Roy Baumeister and colleagues have established that making decisions and choices, taking initiatives and suppressing impulses all seem to draw on the same well of mental energy.

They found that straight after accomplishing a task that required them to use their willpower, people were far more likely to struggle with other willpower-related tasks. Baumeister and colleagues all come to the same conclusion: self-control and willpower can be used up. This has nothing to do with being physically tired. Your self-control decreases and you start to give in to temptation when you are *mentally* exhausted.

Spend the afternoon filling out your tax form or a job application, for example, and even though you have every intention of going for a run, your brain doesn't have enough energy left and is too tired to motivate you. Your resolve goes out the window and you give in to eating chocolate in front of the TV for the rest of the evening. You've lost both your will and your power!

So how can you get more willpower?

Although you may have limited willpower and self-control, it can be increased and strengthened through mental exercise. Just like exercising your muscles to build up your strength. By working on small tasks that you are reluctant or too lazy to do, you can gain inner strength and develop the ability to overcome your mind's resistance. You can actually train your mind to obey you!

Set small daily goals which you would usually rather avoid doing and get them done no matter what.

Try doing one of these things every day for two weeks

- Wash the dishes immediately after every meal.
- Make your bed every morning without fail.
- Cut out a couple of cups of tea or coffee that you normally have at particular times of the day.
- Carry around something tempting. It doesn't need to be for an entire day, but for long enough that you will be truly tempted. By consistently saying 'no', you will increase your ability to resist other temptations.
- Only going up a few floors? Don't take the lift, walk up the stairs.
- Get off the tube or bus one stop earlier or park your car 10 minutes from your destination and walk the rest of the way.
- Focus on sitting up straight every day.
- Change what you say. Say 'hello' instead of 'hi' or 'hey'. Or 'I will' instead of 'I'll' or 'I am' instead of 'I'm'. You'll find it takes willpower to consciously go against your instincts. It doesn't matter how you correct your speech, as long as you change your natural speech habits.

Focus on one small task at a time. Don't do too many things that you don't really want to in any one day. Don't, for example, make yourself wash up, take the rubbish out and skip sugar in your tea all at once. You'll only overload your brain!

'I'm trying to pare down decisions. I don't want to make decisions about what I'm eating or wearing because I have too many other decisions to make.'

Barack Obama

Each decision you make during the day dips into your willpower reserves. Follow Obama's example: cut down the number of decisions you make to a minimum, and focus on the most important ones.

Plan for the times when you know your self-control and willpower are going to be low. For example, if you've got several meetings that will need all your tact and patience *and* you also have to revise for a test or exam, don't expect to make decisions about holiday plans when you get home that evening. Do that instead on a day that you know won't be quite so mentally draining.

When you are able to act 'as if', and make yourself do even the smallest things you don't feel like doing, you will feel more in control and pleased with yourself. This can lead to more positive thinking; for example, 'I can make myself walk up the stairs instead of taking the lift every day – that means I can also make myself go to the gym.'

Seven more ways to stay motivated

1. Refocus on the benefits. Remind yourself of the good reasons – the benefits – of achieving what it is you want to achieve.
2. Listen to music or a podcast while you are working on the steps towards your goal. Go through your personal finances while listening to calming music.
3. Do it with someone else. Things that are difficult to find the enthusiasm to do are especially tedious when doing them alone. So, invite friends over to paint your room and then cook everyone a simple meal or order a curry or pizza. Whatever it is, partner up and get it done!
4. Do it in a different environment. Take your laptop to a café, garden or park and do your work from there.
5. Do it mindfully; move into the present moment instead of searching for ways to avoid it. If you're cleaning, tidying or decorating, for example, do it properly, purposefully and with deliberation. Look for things about what you're doing that you may not have seen before – smells, textures, colours and shapes.
6. Reward yourself for your progress. Before you get started, think of something you'll reward yourself with. This, in itself, sets up something to work towards – a goal. For some tasks, just taking a break and having a cup of tea or coffee might be the goal and the reward. For more demanding tasks, you may want to reward yourself by doing

(Continued)

something even more enjoyable, like going to the cinema or taking a trip to some place nice with friends, or buying yourself something.

7. Still flagging? Another way in which willpower resembles your muscles is that, when its strength is depleted, willpower can be revived with a small sugar hit. Just a piece of chocolate or fruit can reboot your willpower.

Do be aware of when you've used your willpower. Each time you reflect on successful use of your willpower, once again, you're thinking positively.

In a nutshell

- It's normal to be reluctant to get started on something. Be prepared to move through that feeling on your way to achieving what you want.
- Acting 'as if' is a way to create motivation to do something.
- If even the smallest task seems too hard, tell yourself you're just going to do five minutes right now. Make it easy for yourself to get started on the things you do actually want to achieve.
- Once you get going, if you have a plan for the steps you need to take, it makes it easier to move on from one step to the next.
- Don't wait for your feelings to change before you take the action. Just take the action and see how your thoughts and feelings change. It's a positive

feedback loop – acting 'as if' positively influences further thoughts and actions.

- Small changes in how you use your body can add up to a big change in how you feel. If you can keep your mind on maintaining a couple of positive postures consistently, your thoughts, feelings and behaviour can match up.
- Willpower is limited and it is easily used up. But by carrying out simple activities that require *small* amounts of self-control, you will soon develop the self-control and willpower to tackle the bigger issues.
- Plan for the times when you know your self-control and willpower are going to be low. Don't do too many things that you don't really want to in any one day. You'll only overload your brain!

5
Creating a Positive Mindset

You have to choose which way to think. It's a choice. Only you can make that choice. No one can force you to think more positively. But once you do start thinking more positively, it's useful to reinforce positive thoughts and behaviours so that they become a habit.

In this chapter, you can read about a range of ways you can help yourself and train your brain to be more positive.

1. Appreciate your day

'It takes but one positive thought when given a chance to survive and thrive to overpower an entire army of negative thoughts.'

Dr Robert H. Schuller

A simple but powerful way to develop a positive mindset is, at the end of each day, to think of three things that went well. You can simply reflect on what those things are at the end of the day – while you're brushing your teeth or as you go to sleep – or you may want to write down what those three good things were in a notebook.

They only need to be small, simple things; for example, it could be that a friend sent you an encouraging text, or your cat or dog did something amusing and you watched something good on TV. Perhaps for the first time this week, your train arrived on time. Maybe someone told you something you found useful and interesting, you heard a favourite song on the radio and you found something you thought you'd lost.

Noticing what's good really encourages positive thinking, because when you think about the positive events and people in your life, you groove those neural pathways that help to establish positive thinking as a habit.

In fact, if you find it hard to do anything else recommended in this book, if you can just do this – identify three positive things each day – then you're doing something that can really help you turn a corner.

Whether you've had a good day or not, identify and reflect on the small pleasures that happened. Just make an effort every day for a couple of weeks to identify the good things in your day and then think about them for a few minutes. You will soon find yourself actively looking for things to appreciate and, after a while, it will become second nature.

You can find something to make you smile in the simplest of things but it helps if you keep your eyes open for them. Doing this not only helps train your mind to think positively, but if you've not had a good day, you are learning how to identify the positive despite difficulties and disappointments. So yes, you missed the train, for example, but it was a really good cup of coffee that you drank while waiting for the next train, or you received an amusing text from your friend while you waited.

And no, you didn't get offered the job or a place on the course, but at least they did give you some helpful feedback. And although the cinema was full, there were no seats left for the film you wanted to see, you went to a restaurant you hadn't been to before instead and the food was excellent.

2. Be kind

You can further increase your positivity by being positive with other people. The most straightforward way is to be kind to other people and all living things. Being kind and being compassionate creates a positive mindset; it gets you into a cycle of positive thinking and behaviour.

Why? Because when you make an effort to be kind, you have to actively look for opportunities to be kind; to think in positive ways. People appreciate positivity, and the more you share it with others, the more you are practising it in your own life.

If you are caring and supportive to other people, you are likely to get a positive response from them. This will help you feel more positive about yourself and how other people perceive you. Help other people and, in the process, you help yourself.

You may feel you have little to offer, but it only has to be a cup of tea, an invite to dinner or an offer to help someone with a task or chore. You'll lift their spirits and see yourself making a positive difference at the same time.

Plan for kindness; small actions you could take in your daily life. Think about what you might do to show some kindness, then you're more likely to spot opportunities when they come up, when, for example, you notice someone in need. It could be that you give up your seat on the train or bus to someone who needs it more than you. Or that you help someone struggling up the stairs with a baby buggy.

We all have innate kindness and compassion but sometimes it takes a reminder to tune into it. You only need to be a little aware of other people to start seeing opportunities to help. It doesn't have to cost anything or take much time.

What goes around comes around – and with kindness it *really* does. Being kind to others increases your own chances of someone being kind to you.

20 ways to be nice

1. Get in touch with someone you haven't been in contact with for a while. Write them a card, email or text just to let them know you were thinking about them.

2. Send a surprise gift to a friend. When you find something you know a friend would like, don't wait for a birthday or Christmas, send it now.

3. Be thoughtful. Did your colleague have a bad day today? Bring her a coffee tomorrow morning.

4. Let your partner watch their show. And don't roll your eyes or huff and puff about it.

5. Be generous when tipping.

6. Spread the word. If you know someone who decorates or cleans, is a plumber or a gardener and you could recommend them, let others know.

7. Invite people out. Ask someone to do something nice with you – the cinema, a show, a walk, a meal.

8. Respond to texts and emails. Even if you have to say 'Just to let you know I got your email and I'll get back to you later/tomorrow/next week.' People like to know they're not being ignored.

9. In a supermarket queue, let the person who seems rushed go in front of you.

10. Be polite on the road; be kind to other drivers. In a queue, let people merge in.

11. Hold the door open for someone and smile at them as you do.

(Continued)

12. Buy someone a coffee and cake or some fresh fruit – summer strawberries or raspberries. It could be your colleagues, neighbours, family or friends; whoever you choose, surprise them.
13. Don't leave others waiting for you. Be on time.
14. Send a surprise book to someone from an online retailer.
15. Share your skills. If you have a skill – photography, Mexican cooking, website programming, gardening – and someone you know has expressed an interest in what you do, offer to teach them what you know.
16. Offer to help deliver or collect something for someone.
17. Speak out. There are people in our world who need someone to speak out for them. You don't have to take on that cause by yourself, but join others. It could be Amnesty International – a global movement of more than seven million people who take injustice personally – or it could be speaking up at a local council meeting, writing letters or otherwise making a need heard.
18. Contact someone you know who is going through a difficult time. Phone or write them a card, email or text, cook a meal or send flowers or some other thoughtful expression to let them know you care and are thinking about them.
19. Do a chore that you don't normally do for someone else. If your partner always empties the rubbish or the dishwasher, do it for them.

20. Save a life. Donate blood. Donated blood is a lifeline for many people needing long-term treatments, not just in emergencies. Your blood's main components, red cells, plasma and platelets, are vital for many different uses. Go to http://www.blood.co.uk.

Of course, some people are easier to be kind to than others; if they show gratitude or if they have been kind to you first, it's easy to be kind back. It's not easy to be kind to people who are rude and ungrateful. Don't let that put you off; they might not be nice, but you are! And if you can show a kindness it may just make them nicer.

3. Work to help other people

During the 1990s, David Rowntree was the drummer in Blur, the hugely successful British band. But by 2003, his marriage had ended and Blur had disbanded. So David enrolled on an Open University course and, motivated by an urge to help some of society's most blighted people, studied to become a barrister.

He went on to spend one night a week working as a 'Police Station Representative', interviewing and advising people who had been arrested. 'The more I do it, the more important I think it is. By and large, nobody is speaking up for these people. Nobody's on their side. Probably eighty per cent are either drug addicts or have other mental health problems. And society has branded them as evil, so there is no one on their side.'

David is now a solicitor specializing in criminal law. He advises in relation to general criminal defence including police station representation. He is also a patron of Amicus – an organization that provides legal representation for those on Death Row in the United States.

Helping others creates a positive mindset. It gets you into a cycle of positive thinking and behaviour. Doing something to benefit someone else can make both you and the people you are helping feel good. You don't have to make it your career, there's a wide variety of opportunities in voluntary work.

And it's not only people whose situations you can help improve. You can also help animals. Stephanie, for example, started volunteering when she was ten years old.

> We lived near the headquarters of the Cats Protection League. Me and my brother volunteered once a week for 'cat cuddling' – sitting with the cats, stroking them and playing with them to give them exercise.

> I'm 32 now; I love animals and have always had my own cat. Up until recently, I used my professional skills in marketing to help the work of a local cat and rabbit rescue centre. (Yes there is such a thing!)

> Currently, I'm volunteering as a Trainee Guide Dog boarder.

The charity 'Guide Dogs' has found that dogs living with a boarder learn better and make the transition into home life with their new guide dog owner more easily. So, I have a new young dog for 16 weeks. I bring her to the training school each morning, take her home again each evening and look after her at weekends.

Guide Dogs provides all the dog's food, equipment, any vet's bills etc. and I get ongoing support and training around dog care and behaviour from Guide Dogs' staff.

Having my own dog wouldn't be practical as I'm at work all day. But boarding a trainee dog means I get to enjoy part-time doggy company and at the same time know that I'm playing a part in enabling a blind person to be more independent.

If you would like to give some of your time and help to a cause you're interested in, you can volunteer with an organized group. Whether it's supporting adults to learn to read, mentoring young people, supporting ex-offenders, advocating for people with mental health problems or visiting elderly people in hospital, you'll be able to make a difference. A positive difference.

4. Give compliments

Compliments, like kindness and compassion, crystallize positive thinking. Why? Because to give a compliment you first have to think of something positive – to actively look for and comment on other people's good efforts, choices and intentions.

When you give praise, show appreciation or simply say 'thank you' you let the other person know that their efforts or actions have been noticed. So look for ways to compliment people for their character, their choices and their actions.

Ten ways to compliment people

1. Acknowledge other people's qualities – the way they successfully handled a situation, for example: 'I admire that you manage to stay calm whenever a customer is being difficult.'
2. Explain, too, why they made a difference. People feel good if they know that they made a difference. For example, 'I feel like I really learnt something from seeing how you handled that.'
3. Put it in writing. Putting it in writing – an email, text or handwritten note – shows even more effort on your part while also giving the person a permanent reminder of the praise.
4. Make a positive comment on a website or blog. The next time you read something that encourages or motivates you, let the writer know. Let someone know how they helped or inspired you with their book, website or blog. Write a positive review or comment.
5. Do more to create a spirit of positivity with your friends online. The 'like' button on social media makes it too easy to passively acknowledge what you do, in fact, like. Make the effort more often to write a line or two of positive comment to your friends on Facebook.

6. Notice what someone is wearing and how they look.
7. Compliment people on their homes.
8. Be specific – don't just say 'what a nice home' or 'you look nice'. Add what, specifically, is nice – their hairstyle or the furniture they've chosen.
9. Notice the work someone does. It could be someone who serves you in a shop or café. Make a positive comment about their work or business.
10. Praise a parent for their child. When the opportunity arises, compliment someone on the abilities or behaviour of their child.

Take a look around and see who you can pay a compliment to today. If you like something someone has done, don't keep it to yourself. Tell them. You don't need to be an expert to do it well. You just need to be sincere.

Quick positivity triggers

Positivity triggers can give you an instant positivity boost:

1. Collect positive, inspiring quotes, poetry and song lyrics for different situations in your life. Read them when you need a shot of positivity.
2. Listen to (and dance to) upbeat music.
3. Remember someone or something that made you laugh.

(*Continued*)

4. Listen to or watch five minutes of something that makes you laugh. For me, it's TV programmes *Gavin and Stacey*, *Everyone Loves Raymond* and the standup comedians Bill Bailey and Peter Kay.

Some people also find it helpful to keep objects, such as photos or letters that make them feel good. Identify for yourself what you own that sparks joy.

5. Mind your language

Simple tweaks to the words you use can make a big difference to your mindset; to how you think, what you say and do.

'And' not 'but'
Look at these two sentences:

'I went to the shop *but* I forgot to buy the milk.'
'I think your report is great, *but* you should focus more on meeting deadlines.'

'But' is a minimizing word that detracts from the positive thought or statement before it. In this example, by using the word 'but' you've taken away from the fact that you did, nevertheless, buy the other things you needed. In the case of the report, you've minimized the fact that the report *has* been written.

Replacing the word 'but' with 'and' creates a much more positive meaning. By using the word 'and' you make it more likely that you will also come up with a solution. 'But' is final. 'And' infers there's still more to come, as you can read here:

'I went to the shops and I forgot to buy the milk *and* so after lunch I'll go back and buy some.'

'I think your report is great, *and* if you could focus more on meeting deadlines, things really would improve.'

Each time, the word 'and' compels you to complete the sentence in a positive way.

'But' not 'and'

It works the other way round too; in different circumstances, replacing 'and' with 'but' makes a negative sentence more positive. For example, 'I'm so unfit *but* I can exercise and get fitter.' This sentence started out as a negative thought, then got turned into a positive thought.

This time the word 'but' encourages you to complete your sentence with something positive.

In fact, if you could just add a 'but' to every negative thought you produced, you could transform all negative thoughts into positive ones!

'I don't think I'll ever find a partner' becomes 'I don't think I'll ever find a partner *but* if I start going out more, I could meet someone.'

'I'll never pay off this debt' becomes 'I'll never pay off this debt, *but* if I get some expert advice there could be a way to work it out.'
'I don't like living here but ...'
'I'm so fed up with my job but ...'

The more often you can add a 'but' to a negative thought, the more your brain creates neural pathways that build the habit of positive thinking. It's an acceptance and commitment approach; it accepts where you are, but shows you the road ahead.

What negative thought have you had that you can turn into a positive one with the simple use of a 'but'?

'I .... but ....'

Should or could?
Instead of saying 'should' or 'shouldn't' try using 'could' instead. Using the word 'could' instead of 'should' suggests that you do, in fact, have a choice of whether you do something or not. This shift in the use of words is a more positive, flexible approach to thinking and doing things.

Rather than suggesting that someone or something is making or expecting you to do something – which adds pressure that creates more negativity – you are making a choice about what to think and do or not think and do.

Whenever you find yourself saying 'I should', ask yourself 'What would happen if I didn't?' and in response to statements like 'I shouldn't', ask 'What would happen if I did?'

'I should get in touch with that friend I haven't spoken to for ages.'

When you ask 'What would happen if I didn't get in touch?' whatever the answer is, it may prompt you to get in touch – because you do really want to catch up with them – or realize that you aren't really that bothered any more.

Free yourself from doing things you don't want to do by being more aware of sentences that include 'should' and 'shouldn't'.

Listen to the people around you and to people talking on the TV and radio. Be aware of how and when other people use 'should', 'shouldn't', 'can't', 'must' and 'mustn't'. Do their words create a positive or negative approach? Listen out for other people's negative words and phrases and think of positive alternatives.

Never ever and always

Words like 'always' and 'never' are examples of 'all or nothing' thinking. They are words that are often unhelpful because the statements that include them are rarely true. For instance, 'I always forget things' is probably not true. You don't always forget things really, do you? It would be far more realistic to say 'I sometimes forget things'.

Yet

If things aren't happening the way you want them to, simply adding 'yet' to the end of a sentence can create a more positive mindset. Consider, for example, the impact of 'We're not getting any orders' compared to 'We're not getting any orders yet'.

The 'yet' tells you that something hasn't happened up to now but that there's still time; there are still possibilities and opportunities. It encourages you to be hopeful and look for a solution.

'Why' questions

Do you ever ask yourself questions like 'Why does this always happen to me?' 'Why is life so unfair?' 'Why can't I get it right?'

Brooding over questions like these is a guaranteed way to bring yourself down. Instead, turn them into positive, answerable questions, rephrase them into 'how' questions. 'How can I make sure this doesn't happen to me again?' 'How can I make life more fair?' and 'How can I get it right?'

Don't do that!

Telling yourself what you do want rather than what you don't want puts the focus on what you want to happen rather than what you don't. It increases your chances of a positive outcome.

Instead of saying what you *can't* do, say what you *can* do. For example, rather than saying 'I can't do this until tomorrow', a more positive way of saying this would be to simply say 'I can do this tomorrow'.

It's the same with motivating other people; both children and adults. Tell them what you want them to do rather than what you don't want them to do. It's a far more positive message. Rather than saying, for example, 'Don't throw the ball inside!' Say 'Please take the ball outside.'

Talk to yourself
When it comes to motivating yourself, research shows that in a variety of situations, if you address yourself by your own name, your chances of doing well can increase significantly.

It might seem weird, but it can focus your thinking and motivate you. Rather than telling yourself, for example, 'This is what I'm going to do next', address yourself using your name, 'James, this is what you're going to do next.' By using your own name you're distancing yourself from your self. It would appear that this psychological distance encourages self-control, allowing you to think clearly and perform more competently.

Try it!

Be more aware of the words you use. It's perfectly okay to pause and organize your thoughts so that you can phrase your thoughts – and what you say out loud – in a positive way. And if you catch yourself using a negative word or phrase, stop and rephrase what you want to say in more positive terms. Writing letters, emails and texts provides the perfect opportunity to work on positive language, as you can think about and edit your words before sending.

Remember, your self-talk can be positive: kind, encouraging and empowering.

Make the effort to train your brain to think positively and you really will make it more likely that you'll have helpful, positive thoughts and beliefs in all sorts of situations and circumstances.

In a nutshell

- At the end of each day, identify three small positive things that happened. You'll soon find yourself actively looking for things to appreciate and, after a while, it will become a habit. A positive habit.
- Doing this not only helps train your mind to think positively, but if you've not had a good day, you are learning how to identify the positive despite difficulties and disappointments.
- When you make an effort to be kind, you have to actively look for opportunities to be kind; to think in positive ways.
- Volunteering allows you to connect with others in your community and make it a better place. See yourself making a positive difference.
- Compliments, like kindness and compassion, crystallize positive thinking; you have to actively look

for and comment on other people's efforts, choices and good intentions.

- Be more conscious – and conscientious – about the words you use; frame your thoughts in positive words and language.
- Simple tweaks to specific words you use can make a big difference to your mindset; to how you think, what you say and do.
- When you're aiming to motivate yourself, if you address yourself by your own name, your chances of doing well can increase significantly.
- The more you train your brain to think positively, the more likely you'll have helpful, positive thoughts and beliefs.

6
Building Your Self-Esteem and Confidence

When faced with a new challenge or opportunity, do you lack confidence and think to yourself 'I can't do that' or 'I'll fail' or 'I won't be any good at this' or 'I'm stupid and hopeless'? Or do you think 'I'm going to give this a good try' or 'I could do well at this' or 'I'll try my best'.

Your confidence and self-esteem have quite an impact on your ability to get what you want and achieve your goals. Confidence, though, is not about what you can or can't do, it's what you *think* and *believe* you can or can't do.

If you've ever failed or struggled to cope with a particular situation in the past, you may *believe* it will be difficult or that you'll fail if you try to do it again. And if you've got something coming up that's new to you and that you're unsure about, you may talk yourself out of it with negative self-talk, *believing* that you 'can't' or 'won't' be able to do something.

Negative thinking and cognitive distortions such as jumping to conclusions, catastrophizing and tunnel thinking can undermine your confidence and can make you believe that you can't do certain things.

But many of us have grown up allowing ourselves to mostly say and believe negative things about ourselves. Thinking otherwise would be seen as 'big headed' or 'showing off'. Too often, you can think that you're not good enough and even when you do something well, you can tend to think more about mistakes you made than what you achieved.

As well as undermining your confidence, negative self-talk can also knock your self-esteem, making you feel bad about yourself and your abilities. If you have low self-esteem, your thoughts and beliefs about yourself will often be negative.

There are a number of reasons why you might think negatively about yourself and your abilities. It could be a change in your life which results in how you see and value yourself; the end of a relationship, illness and disability or being unemployed, for example, can all lower your self-esteem. Feeling 'different' – finding it hard to relate to others, comparing yourself to others or being criticized, humiliated, bullied, discriminated against or left out by others – can also leave you feeling like you have little worth. If you are under a lot of stress and finding it hard to cope, or you have overly high standards and high expectations for yourself, this too can lead to negative thinking about yourself.

Whatever the reason, the result is often the same; a stream of negative thoughts that convince you that you can't do something and that you're no good.

The problem with thinking you're no good, though, is that you behave as if it's true; low self-esteem can influence what you do or don't do in ways that confirm that you *aren't* able to do things or *aren't* very good. Feel bad about yourself because you believe you're not academic, for example, and you're unlikely to attempt anything that looks like formal study. And because you don't attempt any academic, formal study, you never find out if, in fact, with the right teaching and support, you are actually capable.

On the other hand, when your self-esteem is high, your thoughts and beliefs about yourself are positive; you feel good about your abilities and you're more likely to believe that you *can* do things and they will either turn out reasonably well or, if they don't, that you'll be able to cope. This time it's a helpful, positive dynamic where each positive aspect feeds into the other.

Start from a position of strength

So, how to reverse an unhelpful dynamic? The best place to start building your confidence and self-esteem is from a position of strength. Instead of focusing on what you believe you can't do, focus on what you *know* you *can* do and what you know makes you feel good about yourself. There are a number of ways you can do this.

Focus on the things that make you feel good about yourself

Think about the aspects of your life that matter to you, that you enjoy doing and do reasonably well. Those areas could be related to, for example, your work, family, friends, hobbies and interests and sports. They will be activities where you know what you're doing and like doing it.

Doing something that you enjoy, and that you are good at, can help build your confidence and increase your self-esteem. Why? Because you not only *believe* these are things you like and do OK at, you *know* it too. When you reflect on the activity; when you think back over what you're doing and have been doing, you have positive thoughts about the activity and about yourself; you feel good about yourself.

Dean, for example, is 34. One aspect of his life that's important to him is sport. In particular, football is important. It's something he enjoys and does quite well in. He feels confident and good about himself when he plays football. His friends are important too. Keeping in touch with his friends, doing things together and supporting each other is something he enjoys and is good at.

Chaya is a lawyer. She's good at her job and enjoys it. What really makes her feel good, though, is the voluntary work she does once a week with homeless young people. Chaya feels that she's really able to help the young people by listening and providing advice and information.

Whenever you enjoy and do well in an area of your life that matters to you, you can feel good about yourself. You don't have to excel at an activity, you just need to like it and be good enough at it.

What do you like doing? What do you enjoy? Maybe it's your job or an aspect of your job. Perhaps it's voluntary work that you do. Maybe it's an interest like cooking or baking, fishing, gardening or dancing.

Are there activities in your life that bring you a sense of satisfaction? Make yourself aware of what those activities are so that you can develop your confidence and self-esteem from a position of strength. Find what you enjoy doing and do more of it.

Perhaps you have a natural ability to do something well. Maybe there's something that you have always wanted to learn. Find an interest or activity that will not challenge you too much to begin with so that you can feel you have achieved something and have a chance to build your confidence.

In Chapter 3 you'll have read about working towards and achieving goals. Doing this – working towards and achieving things – can also help you develop your self-esteem and confidence. Each step that you successfully achieve provides the evidence that enables you to believe that you *are* doing well and you *can* succeed.

Be sure to reflect on what you've done afterwards. Doing so results in a triple blessing; each time you *think* about doing something enjoyable, then actually *do* it and then *reflect* on it, your brain has strengthened those positive neural pathways three times.

Identify your qualities

Another way to feel good about yourself and what you are able to do is to identify your personal qualities, distinctive characteristics and attributes. Read through this list and as you do, tick *each and every* quality that applies to you.

Adaptable	Good natured	Perceptive
Adventurous	Hardworking	Practical
Calm	Helpful	Precise
Caring	Honest	Realistic
Conscientious	Imaginative	Reassuring
Cooperative	Independent	Reliable
Courteous	Innovative	Resilient
Creative	Intuitive	Resourceful
Curious	Likeable	Responsible
Decisive	Logical	Sense of Humour
Dependable	Loyal	Sincere
Determined	Methodical	Sociable
Diplomatic	Meticulous	Sympathetic
Empathic	Observant	Tactful
Encouraging	Optimistic	Thorough
Energetic	Organized	Tidy
Fair	Outgoing	Tolerant
Firm	Patient	Trustworthy
Flexible	Persistent	Truthful
Friendly	Objective	Understanding
Gentle	Open-minded	

Now choose your top five qualities; the five that you think best describe you.

Next, for each quality, write a sentence or two that describes how and why you are like this.

For example, if you felt that patience was one of your qualities, you might say, 'I can calmly wait for things to happen in their own time. I am patient with colleagues who take a while longer to get things done.'

If another of your qualities was persistence, you might say, 'I can keep going with a task, especially in the face of difficulties. I overcome setbacks and carry on. I did this recently when insisting on the specific health care I felt I needed.'

And if being reliable was one of your qualities, you might have written, 'I can be trusted and depended on to do what I say I will. Friends have told me how much they value this about me.'

Ask yourself questions to help you to write about your good qualities:

- How have I helped someone by having this quality?
- What challenges have I overcome by having this quality?
- How has this quality helped me in my work or day-to-day life?

When you have low feelings of self-worth, your negative thoughts distort your perception of yourself and you overlook the positives. Identifying your good qualities and explaining how, why and when you have each quality can help you to see your own worth and so contribute to good self-esteem.

Acknowledge your positive qualities and the things you are good at. Get into the habit of identifying and thinking positive things about yourself and create your own personal affirmations.

Personal affirmations

You may have come across the idea of positive affirmations before. An affirmation is simply a positive statement that is true. The sort of affirmations you may have read or heard about are usually statements such as:

* I live in the present and am confident of the future
* I feel safe in the rhythm and flow of life
* My outer self is matched by my inner well-being
* Nothing is impossible and life is great.

All well and good, but for an affirmation to be most effective for you, it's got to be specifically about you; it has to be personal and believable to you. With the exercise above – where you identify a personal quality and describe how and why you are like this – you create your own personal affirmations. These personal affirmations are more likely to be effective for you *because* they are personal. So, create your own personal affirmations – write them down and keep them where you can read them as and when you need to.

Positive people

'Surround yourself with people who make you happy. People who make you laugh, who help you when you're in need. People who genuinely care. They are the ones worth keeping in your life. Everyone else is just passing through.'

Karl Marx

Self-esteem and confidence come from two sources. They come from what you believe about yourself and how you value yourself. They also come from what other people appear to believe about you and how they value you.

Throughout your life you come across all kinds of people; different in many ways. But when it comes to how they impact on your self-esteem and confidence, other people can fall into one of two camps; they're either 'radiators' or 'drains'.

People who are radiators spread warmth and positivity, while drains can leave you feeling irritated and upset, disappointed or angry, guilty or resentful. They drain your energy. Their misery, criticism and complaining overwhelm you with their negativity.

Who you spend most of your time with can make a big difference to the way you think, feel and behave. You need radiators in your life! Positive people are likely to respond to you in positive ways and so make you think positively about yourself and the world around you.

If you have low self-esteem, there might be people close to you who, deliberately or not, encourage the negative beliefs and opinions that you hold about yourself. It's important to identify these people and take action to stop them from doing this.

Tiny frogs

There was once a bunch of tiny frogs, who arranged a running competition. The goal was to run, hop and jump to the top of a very high tower. A big crowd gathered around the tower to see the race and cheer on the contestants.

The race began. No one in the crowd really believed that the tiny frogs would reach the top of the tower. They shouted 'It's too difficult!!! They will NEVER make it to the top' and 'Not a chance. The tower is too high.'

The tiny frogs began collapsing, one by one, except for those who were managing to climb higher. The crowd continued to yell 'It's too difficult! It's much too hard. No one will make it!'

More tiny frogs got tired and gave up. But one continued higher and higher. This one wouldn't give up! And he reached the top. Everyone wanted to know how this one frog managed such a great feat.

His secret? This little frog was deaf!!

Author Unknown

It is not always possible or practical to switch off from negative people or remove them from your life completely. What you can do, however, is reduce the amount of time you spend around them and increase the amount of time you spend with 'radiators', the positive people in your life.

Who are the positive people in your life?

Which people come to mind from the questions below?

- Someone I can call on in a crisis
- Someone who makes me feel good about myself
- Someone I can totally be myself with
- Someone who values my opinion
- Someone who tells me how well I am doing
- Someone I can talk to if I am worried
- Someone who really makes me stop and think about what I am doing
- Someone who makes me laugh and I can have fun with
- Someone who shares an interest or hobby with me
- Someone who introduces me to new ideas, interests or new people
- Someone who is generous with their time, ideas or resources.

You may have a different person or a number of people for each situation, or the same one or two people might fit a number of situations. Think widely; the positive people on your list do not just have to be friends or family; they could be colleagues or neighbours.

The person you can talk to if you're worried, for example, could be a professional person that you see such as your GP, a counsellor or someone from an organization with a helpline. Maybe the person who introduces you to new ideas and interests is a documentary maker like David Attenborough. Perhaps there's someone on the radio or TV who makes you laugh. The person who inspires you could be someone you have read about who has overcome adversity or who has achieved something despite all the odds.

In fact, role models are another source of positivity. Role models are people who possess positive characteristics and qualities that inspire us. We all look for different things in a role model but often they are people who practise what they preach and who are willing to act on their beliefs and values. Role models behave ethically and honestly. They show respect for others. Role models are often a source of inspiration because they have overcome adversity in their lives in some way; usually by being persistent or by finding creative solutions to problems and difficulties. We admire people like this!

Positive news
As well as minimizing contact with negative people, minimize the amount of negative news in your life. While staying up to date on important stories can keep you informed, shape your opinions and enable you to take

part in discussions, in an age of information overload, your life can be filled with irrelevant or unnecessary information in an instant.

You're rarely better informed, your life isn't any better and you rarely feel better about yourself, other people or the world around you for having read low-level negative information.

In fact, low-quality information is to the mind what sugar is to the body: empty calories that give you a rush but then bring you down and leave you feeling like crap. You wouldn't want to stuff your body with low-quality food. Why cram your mind with low-quality thoughts?

Circles of Concern vs. Circles of Control   In his book, *The Seven Habits of Highly Effective People*, Stephen Covey explains the concept of the 'Circle of Concern' and the 'Circle of Influence'. The Circle of Concern is the area that we have no control over but that we can waste time and energy getting caught up in; getting wound up and worried about.

A wide range of events – the economy, for example, war and terrorism, the behaviour of celebrities and political scandal – fall into the Circle of Concern. You have little or no control over these events but can easily consume more and more information about them. This drains your time and energy and can leave you feeling stressed, helpless and negative simply *because* you have little or no control over these events.

The Circle of Influence, on the other hand, is the area that you do have control over. It involves the issues and events that you *can* influence in your daily life.

If you turn your attention to the Circle of Influence, you turn to an area where you have more control and influence. Your goals, your attitude, the skills you develop, what you learn, what you read, listen to and watch, what you eat, the amount of exercise you take and so on. You can do something about the issues and events in the Circle of Influence. When you give most of your time and energy to your Circle of Influence, you are likely to feel more positive about yourself because you can initiate and influence change.

Most of us have a number of sources of information that we could eliminate from our lives with no detriment to our lives whatsoever. Instead of consuming whatever is readily available, and drains you, step into the Circle of Influence and make more conscious choices about what you read, watch and listen to. Look for stories about people that inspire you. Don't read about people who are portrayed as victims; where the focus is on the unfairness of their situation and nothing seems to get resolved.

Instead, read and listen to stories about people who have coped with adversity. What was it that helped them cope and bounce back? Was it their ability to find the positive in adversity? You need positive role models in your life, so watch and read motivational stories or speeches. TED talks (www.ted.com), for example, are inspiring, educational and motivating.

Online, you can find websites dedicated to sharing inspiring and positive news from around the world:

www.dailygood.org/
www.huffingtonpost.com/good-news/
www.goodnewsnetwork.org/
http://positivenews.org.uk/
www.sunnyskyz.com/

So steer clear of negative headlines and dire tales of things going wrong. Look, instead, for uplifting stories that celebrate the best of life and be inspired by the good in the world around us.

In a nutshell

- Confidence is not what you can or can't do. It's what you *believe* you can or can't do.
- Negative thinking and cognitive distortions undermine your confidence and self-esteem, making you feel bad about yourself and your abilities.
- When your self-esteem is high, your thoughts about yourself are positive; you feel good about your abilities, you're more likely to believe that you *can* do things and that you can manage difficulties. It's a positive dynamic where each aspect feeds into the other.
- Doing something that you enjoy, and that you are good at, can help build your confidence and increase your self-esteem. So find what you enjoy doing and do more of it.

- Get into the habit of identifying and thinking positive things about yourself and create your own personal affirmations.
- Minimize the amount of negative people and negative news in your life. Look for positive stories and news about people that inspire you.
- Focus on your 'Circle of Influence'. When you give most of your time and energy to your Circle of Influence, you are likely to feel more positive, because you can initiate and influence change.

PART 3

Positive Thinking for Difficult Situations

7
Dealing with Disappointments and Setbacks, Trauma and Tragedy

Setbacks and disappointments

It's easy to stay positive when things are going well in your life. The real challenge to positive thinking comes when problems, setbacks and disappointments occur. Unexpected financial difficulties or health problems, other people blocking you or withdrawing their support, for example, can easily set you back.

Being turned down for a place on a course, a TV talent show, a job, flat or house are all sources of disappointment. So are seeing your team lose, bad weather upsetting your plans, failing an exam, or a meeting at work or a social occasion not going as well as you'd planned.

Even if you're trying to forget about it, a disappointment can stay hovering in the back of your mind like a grey cloud. This is a perfectly natural response to the hurt and sadness that occurs when your expectations or hopes fail to materialize.

Whenever a situation leaves you feeling disappointed, you need to sit with it; to take time to acknowledge and accept that what has happened *has* happened and nothing can change that. It's not wrong to feel disappointment.

'When we push away part of us that feels that way, it creates a fragmented self with an acceptable me and unacceptable me.'

Tina Gilbertson

If you're upset or disappointed about something, it's not because you're not positive enough. It's because you're human. If you take an 'acceptance and commitment' approach (as described in Chapter 2) then you can acknowledge and accept you feel like you do, learn from your disappointment and move on.

'Crying has the power to unify our thoughts, feelings and physical body in a way that is cathartic and automatically grounds us in the present.'

Rachel Kelly

It's not always easy to move on though. Negative thinking, dwelling on what failed to materialize – the place on the course, for example, or the sale that didn't go through or the dress that didn't fit – can keep you stuck and unable to move past the disappointment.

But all the time you allow yourself to brood on what did or didn't happen, you make it difficult to move forward, to think logically and clearly – to think positively.

Sports fans and people who take part in a sport know that whenever they or their team lose they can't stay disappointed for long. They know that staying disappointed gets them nowhere. They let go of negative thinking and instead move on to think about the next game or race and the opportunities it will present.

In order to leave disappointment behind, you must do the same; make a decision that you are going to move on. It won't happen automatically; you have to actively look for something positive about the situation.

In his 2005 Stanford University graduation address, for example, Steve Jobs explained what happened after he was fired from Apple.

> I didn't see it then, but it turned out that getting fired from Apple was the best thing that could have ever happened to me. The heaviness of being successful was replaced by the lightness of being a beginner again, less sure about everything. It freed me to enter one of the most creative periods of my life. During the next five years, I started a company named NeXT, another company named Pixar, and fell in love with an amazing woman who would become my wife. I'm pretty sure none of this would have happened if I hadn't been fired from Apple.

Like Steve Jobs, you can always draw out something good from a disappointment.

When was the last time that you were disappointed? What did you learn? Did you even stop to reflect on this? Positive thinkers see disappointment as a signal that they need to adjust their expectations and hopes; to rethink their plans so that they can get back on course to achieve what it is that they want to achieve.

For example, supposing you had put a lot of time and effort into studying and revising for an exam. You expected to pass with flying colours. But you failed; you fell short of your expectations. What you originally thought you needed to do – the topics you revised, the time and effort and level of understanding – you now know wasn't enough.

Disappointment shows you that you may need to increase your resources or change your approach to achieve the results you want. Your disappointment is actually helping you to move towards your goal, not away from it.

Your experience has resulted in learning something – whether about yourself, another person, the situation or even the world – and responding accordingly. Learning from failure involves reflecting on what happened, identifying what went wrong and working out what needs to change in order to avoid and prevent similar disappointments and setbacks in the future.

Be aware that whenever you are able to adapt, you create the possibility of happiness and success that doesn't depend on perfect conditions.

For example, there was much criticism about lack of black nominees and winners at the 2016 BRITs ceremony. But funk singer songwriter George Clinton had a different perspective on the controversy. 'It's always been that way, but it only makes you have to work harder and get better. That's what it takes to become great – adversity. Things are always changing for the better. Fault is easy to find – but finding a reason to keep on pushing is the hardest thing. And when I can find that reason, I'm satisfied.'

You might need to adjust your expectations but that doesn't always mean that you have to lower your expectations. A few years ago I had an idea for a magazine article on the subject of how to be resilient. I pitched it to several editors but none of them was interested. Once I'd got over my disappointment, I decided that even though magazine editors weren't interested in my idea, book editors might be. Together with my friend Sue, I approached publishers and we were commissioned to write our first book! *(Bounce. Use the power of resilience to live the life you want.)*

Any person who has succeeded or achieved something has faced some disappointments. They learn from their disappointments and move forward – sometimes in a different direction. Active problem-solving allows you to gain a feeling of control and think positively.

Focus on thinking about what can be done rather than what can't be done, and be open to new ideas and new ways of doing things. Rather than thinking, 'I should/shouldn't have ...' try saying 'It might help to ...' or 'I could ...' or 'now I'm going to ...'

Release yourself from your expectation of how things should be. It's too easy to remain disappointed if you're still attached to how things 'should' have been. These expectations are disempowering because, as long as you are trapped in them, they are preventing you from acting constructively on your situation. Dealing with disappointment requires you to adjust or let go of your expectations.

Continue to have goals. Let them drive you forward. As Friedrich Nietzsche said, 'What doesn't kill us makes us stronger.' And that's positive thinking!

Trauma and tragedy

You can always find something positive in a disappointment or setback, but what if a major trauma or tragedy happens?

When you're going through the kind of event that devastates your life, that overwhelms you with shock and grief, the last thing you can think about is being positive.

It may seem an affront to suggest thinking positively when tragedy strikes but it *can* help you to cope with the pain you are facing. The two stories that follow show how two individual people have found positive aspects to trauma and tragedy.

One day in June 2007, Garry Methven finished work and went to the pub to drink, as he did every day. Returning home a few hours later, he was rushing to catch the last tube train home and fell down the escalators. 'I was drunk, so I must have tripped and fallen, and I ended up in a heap on the floor at the bottom.' Garry sustained a serious brain injury.

> I went to rehab, which probably helped, but I couldn't talk properly; I just couldn't find the right words. It's called aphasia. I couldn't go back to work. I had epileptic fits every day. They were terrible, violent – I'd be on the floor, couldn't move my body, couldn't talk, and I would be depressed for ages afterwards.

> Finally I found a charity called Headway East London, which helps people with brain injuries. At first, I would go to the centre and just sit in the corner and not talk to anybody; but then I met people who were in a similar predicament, and who understood what I was going through.

> Although it was a very bad accident, it turned out also to be quite a good accident. I used to be a big drinker; I would wake up in the morning and have vodka before work, then a few pints at lunch in the pub, and then more after work.

> But epilepsy and alcohol don't mix, so I had to give up after my accident. In fact, I'd probably be in more trouble

now if it hadn't happened. I was really selfish before, and I used to cheat on everyone. I'm a lot kinder now that I'm sober.

I live on my own in sheltered housing in London, and I'm much happier now. I haven't had a fit for several months, and although I still have aphasia, it's not as bad as it used to be. I've got a garden, so I'm often out and about, thinking about what I can plant. I don't think about my future, I focus on each day as I live it.

I do think about my daughter's future. She's at university – she's amazingly intelligent. She's such a blessing. I hope she will have a good and happy life. That's the most important thing for me now.

* * * * * * * * * * * *

In 2008, Andrew Foster's brother Christopher shot dead his wife Jill and their 15-year-old daughter Kirstie before setting fire to their Shropshire home and killing himself. Andrew set up a trust fund in his niece's name, for Riding for the Disabled. 'We're trying to get something good out of this', he told reporters.

Finding something positive doesn't mean denying how tragic and devastating the situation is, but it can help prevent you from being overwhelmed by the awfulness of it.

Just as with a disappointment, with trauma, tragedy and grief, you will need to give yourself time to acknowledge and accept that what has happened *has* happened.

Sadness and disappointment, shock and grief are intended to slow you down and allow you to reflect and take in what has happened; to realize that there's no turning back; nothing and no one can change what has happened.

Then, at some point, when you can, focusing on who has been helpful and supportive and what has been a blessing can begin to steer your mind in a positive direction.

Look for the positive

'If you are going through hell, keep going.'
Winston Churchill

Even during the worst of times, there can be something to be thankful for.

In Chapter 5 you will have read about identifying and reflecting on two or three positive things that happened in your day.

If you can get into the habit of doing this in your normal daily life, you will have established those neural pathways that will serve you well when you are faced with really tough times and serious adversity.

In every situation, there is something positive and good. Most of the time it's not obvious. You have to look, and often you have to look hard. But you can help yourself to cope better in difficult times by training yourself to look for the positive in your everyday life.

Nat cared for his Mum who was ill for 18 months before she died. He says:

> I could only see all the bad things – the distress and pain Mum was in, how caring for her had narrowed my life and that my brother did very little to help. I just went with it, it didn't even occur to me that there might be some positive aspects to the situation.
>
> A friend told me about the concept of identifying and reflecting two or three positive things at the end of each day. I put a note next to the bathroom mirror to remind me. It didn't take long to get into the habit.
>
> Now, when I'm faced with a difficult or challenging situation, I think to myself, 'What's good about this?' No matter how bad the situation might seem, it's quite easy for me to find some good things. It doesn't change what's happened but it does help me not to be overwhelmed by it.

Identifying the good things that have happened every day is what people who pray do each evening when they thank God for the blessings of the day. You don't have to be religious to do this. You just need to make it something you do on a regular basis and know that it can help you feel good at the end of each day and prepare you to cope in difficult, challenging times.

Bullying and abuse

However, finding the positive in adversity doesn't mean you should put up with a bad, risky or harmful situation just because you can find some positive aspects to it.

If you're in a relationship or a friendship where you are becoming more and more unhappy and miserable, if you're being bullied or even abused by a colleague, family member or neighbour, you mustn't use positive thinking as an excuse to stay in a bad situation.

You may, for example, be staying in an abusive relationship because you reason that despite the awfulness of it, it's the right thing to do for the children; they will be better off coming from an intact family than from a divorced one and at least you have two incomes coming in. Or, maybe you've convinced yourself that the positive aspect is that your partner isn't bad all the time – most of the time he or she is good fun and you get on well.

This is not positive thinking. It's delusional thinking. Positive thinking does not mean ignoring real difficulties. If someone is persistently badgering, dominating or intimidating you, someone is continually coercing and threatening you, criticizing or humiliating you, tyrannizing you or making abusive remarks and insulting you, you *must* do something. This person will not go away!

Shift your perspective; use positive thinking to think about the good things that can happen if you do what you know to be the right thing; and that is to get out of the relationship.

See leaving a bully or abusive person as a goal. An urgent goal.

Positive people

Staying silent and telling no one will only isolate you while at the same time empowering the bully or abuser so you must get help and support. Don't be afraid to do this. There are people who can give you support and advice, especially if they've been in a similar situation. There are organizations that specialize in supporting anyone who is being bullied or abused. There's a list of websites at the back of this book for support and information in cases of bullying and abuse.

As well as getting help, support and advice, you need to leave as soon as possible; leave the job, the relationship. Walking away is the best thing to do, for in doing so, you put yourself in a positive position: one of being in control. You take away the opportunity for the bully or abuser to continue their behaviour.

Of course, you might have to walk away from a good job, financial stability, a nice home etc. but focus on the positive; that you've left the bully or abuser behind. Once you have left them you can put your energy into finding a new job or somewhere to live instead of spending your energy trying to please, pacify or avoid the bully or abuser.

You *do* have a choice about how to respond. Think positively; think about keeping yourself safe and sane and moving forward towards a better life.

Courage

You'll need courage. Courage feels a lot like fear. But courage is the ability to face difficulty *despite* your fear and concerns. Courage gives you the ability to do something that frightens you. It's strength in the face of hostility or intimidation.

'It's not the size of the dog in the fight, it's the size of the fight in the dog.'

Mark Twain

Whether it's leaving your job or a relationship, standing up for yourself or someone else, public speaking or performing, courage is what makes you brave and helps you move forward.

Positive thinking is inherent in courage; it's an inseparable aspect of courage. It's thinking 'I *can* do this' or 'I *will* do this' and 'I *can* cope and I *can* manage'.

Don't think that you can't be courageous because you don't *feel* courageous. Courage often requires that you act 'as if' you're confident, whatever you actually feel. It's feeling the fear and doing it anyway. It's an exponential process – you only have to start the process; start acting with courage, start with a small step and your courage will increase at a steady rate.

Tap in to your courage. Think of a situation when you felt afraid, yet faced your fear and took action and things turned out OK. What helped? What did other people do or say that helped give you courage? What did you think or feel?

Now, think of a situation you are currently facing that scares you or makes you feel anxious. What are you most afraid of? You might, for example, be afraid of jeopardizing your job if you complain about someone else's behaviour. You might be afraid of telling someone how you feel or you might be anxious about telling someone what you do and don't want to happen in a particular situation.

Remind yourself that you have been courageous before and you *can* summon up your courage again. That's positive thinking!

Focusing on why you're doing something and what you want to achieve, keeping that in your mind, can help prevent feelings of doubt, uncertainty and fear creeping in, because you're thinking positively. Have courage and you open up all sorts of possibilities.

'Life shrinks or expands in proportion to one's courage.'
Anaïs Nin

Criticism

We've all heard of 'constructive' criticism but if you're like most people, you rarely respond positively to even the most well-meant of criticisms. At best, we interpret a criticism as a negative judgement on our thoughts and behaviour and at worst, we receive criticism as a personal attack.

Of course, it doesn't feel great to be told you're not doing, looking, talking or behaving as someone else thinks you should. Criticism can cause you stress and upset and trigger the sort of negative thinking that erodes your self-esteem and confidence.

In some cases, the criticism isn't fair and has more to do with the other person's issues and expectations. It's not a criticism, it's verbal abuse – insulting, offensive and entirely damaging. But in other cases, the criticism is warranted; it's something you may need to consider and act on.

How can you tell the difference between criticism and verbal abuse? Verbal abuse fails to provide any pointers as to what it is that you can improve on. As in this example: 'You're a f***ing idiot – a waste of time and space – you never get things right.' Criticism, on the other hand, describes behaviour that can be improved on. For example, 'This is not what I asked you to do. You haven't done it in the right way.'

If it's a genuine criticism, you can learn from it. Take the case of Luke, who is a successful TV actor. Luke describes a sharp lesson that he learnt early on in his career, in managing criticism:

> I remember when, in my late teens, before I went on to drama school, I was in a local theatre group. This one time, the director was giving me feedback after a scene in front of the whole group. But she couldn't get through a single sentence without me making excuses and contradicting her.
>
> After a few minutes of this, someone spoke up and said, 'Stop talking. You're embarrassing yourself.' It was harsh, but I realized it needed saying and that instead of being defensive, I needed to take on board the director's feedback.

Criticism isn't always delivered gently. A lot of the feedback we receive is not asked for and doesn't come from teachers. Or maybe all of it does. Maybe there's something to learn from every criticism. We just need to be willing to listen, decide if there's any truth in it and then act on it.

Typically, if you're like most people, you see praise as good and criticism as bad. There is, though, a different way of seeing criticism; you can see things in less black and white terms and recognize that although being on the receiving end of criticism isn't easy, it's often a fair reflection of how another person sees you at that point.

How to handle criticism positively
Although other people might not be skilled at giving criticism, you can learn how to handle it and respond to criticism more positively.

Start by listening. Stop and really listen to what the other person is saying.

Imagine, for example, that someone said this to you: 'You're so disorganized! You always forget to do what I've asked you to do. You constantly fail to meet deadlines and you never let anyone know what you're doing or where you are.'

That's some criticism! Could any of it be true? Even if the other person is having a bad day or is known to be critical about everyone and everything, could there be some truth in their remarks?

Often, you can react so quickly to their hostility and exaggerations that you don't stop to consider that there might be some truth in what's being said. Hearing someone tell you that you're '*so* disorganized', '*always* forget', '*constantly* fail' and '*never* let anyone know' can easily put you on the defensive; particularly if it shines a light on your own insecurities. But there is usually some truth in criticism.

Clarify the problem and the solution. If you're not clear about what the critic is accusing you of, rephrase what they've said in your own words. 'I just want to be clear, are you saying ...' or 'I'm not sure I've understood, do you think ...?'

Once you're both clear what the problem is, if they haven't said so already, ask the other person what they think the solution is. Doing this is important because you're making a genuine attempt at finding out how the other person thinks that you can put things right and improve the situation. (You don't have to agree with their solution though.)

Having listened, clarified and asked what they want you to do about it, you slow the exchange down, which gives you time to respond positively; it gives you time to consider what the critic is saying, decide whether it's fair and valid and what your response will be.

You may agree or disagree that certain aspects of their criticism are valid. So, in the example above, you might respond by saying: 'I don't agree that I'm disorganized and always forget what you want me to do. But yes, I do sometimes fail to meet deadlines (there are reasons for this) and yes, I often don't let people know where I am or what I'm doing. I'm sorry. I'll do something about that. I'll do what you suggest and …'

Criticism opens you up to other people's perspectives and interpretations of you – what you think, say and do. OK, it might not all be accurate and the other person may be harsh and exaggerated (critics often are when they're upset, frustrated or angry) but you need to look for seeds of truth in criticism.

It's not easy to take an honest look at yourself and admit that you've done something wrong. But it's OK to have flaws. It's part of being human. If you can admit weaknesses and work on them without putting yourself down, you'll strengthen your ability to handle a variety of situations in positive ways.

And if you honestly feel that their criticism is unfair and invalid, say so. Calmly tell the other person that you understand that that's their perspective and explain how or why their criticism is unfair or plain wrong. Or say nothing and let it go. Most likely their mind is already made up and if you try to argue you will just be adding fuel to the fire.

You don't have much control over what other people say to you. But you can control whether you respond to it by lashing out, arguing, becoming defensive or crumpling and whether or not you learn from it and move on.

Forgiving

Has someone else been the cause of your disappointment, setback or trauma? Maybe it was a parent who let you down when you were young, a partner who was unfaithful? Perhaps it was a friend or colleague who failed you in some way? Whoever and whatever it was, after your initial disappointment, shock or anger has passed, you're presented with a new challenge: do you forgive the person?

Forgiveness means letting go of the resentment, frustration or anger that you feel as a result of someone else's actions. It involves no longer wanting punishment, revenge or compensation. It means recognizing that you have already been hurt once, so you don't need to let the offence, the hurt and pain keep hurting and distressing you by holding on to it.

All the time you feel unable to forgive, you're holding on to something that happened days, weeks, months or even years ago. But you deserve to be free of this negativity! Forgiveness is, first and foremost, for *your* benefit, not the person who hurt or offended you. Forgiveness is for *your* peace of mind.

If you forgive someone, you don't change the past, you change the future. Not forgiving is like deliberately keeping a wound open – it remains raw and it festers. On the other hand, when you forgive, you allow yourself to heal.

So if it's something you do for yourself and if it can help you heal, why is it so hard to forgive? It's hard because you're angry, confused, feel victimized or filled with thoughts of retribution or revenge. It can also be hard to forgive because you simply don't know how to resolve the situation.

If you've now reached a point where you want to put your own or someone else's actions behind you and move on with your life, there are a number of steps you can take.

Firstly, it really helps to accept what has happened and how it affected you. No doubt the other person is responsible for their actions and you wish that what they did had never happened. But you can't change what has already happened. It is what it is.

'Give up on all hope of a better past.'

Matt Child

Think positively: instead of thinking about how you can get back at the other person, think about what you learned from the experience. What would you do differently to avoid becoming involved in a similar situation? Ask yourself 'What strengths can I develop from this?'

Identify any positive aspects. Maybe other people were helpful and supportive when this person betrayed you, hurt or offended you. Maybe, if you've now cut this person from your life, you realize how much better off you are without them.

Change the story you replay to yourself and to other people. Each time you go back over what happened, you access negative thoughts and images. Change your story to one that tells of your decision to forgive; to accept and learn from what happened, to identify any positive aspects and move on. Look to the future; think of creating new, good memories to replace old, bad ones.

Forgiveness doesn't mean you shouldn't have any more feelings about the situation. It doesn't mean you are excusing the other person's actions; it doesn't mean there is nothing further to work out in the relationship or that everything is OK now.

By forgiving, you are accepting what happened and finding a way to live in a state of resolution with it. It may happen quite quickly or it may be a gradual process.

You might find it helpful to write an honest, emotional letter telling the other person how hurt and angry you are. Then tear it up and burn it. As you watch the smoke rise, imagine it carrying your hurt and disappointment into the air; let it go.

Forgiveness puts the final seal on what happened that hurt you. You will still remember what happened, but you will no longer be bound by it.

Guilt and regret

Although feelings of guilt or shame can be distressing, remember that, like all emotions, guilt has a positive intent; to prompt you to put right a decision or action by you that has hurt or offended someone else. If, for example, you felt guilty about having pulled out of a friend's special occasion, then your guilt can prompt you to make it up to her in some way.

If you never felt remorse or guilt, how could you ever care about how your actions could affect others? Guilt only becomes a negative, harmful emotion when you allow it to overwhelm you with shame or self-loathing. Or if you allow it to paralyse you so that you fail to take positive action.

Parenthood, for example, seems to bring a lot of guilty feelings with it. You can feel guilty when you've been irritated and impatient with your children, or when you don't spend as much time with them as you think you should, if you miss a school performance or a meeting with their teacher and so on.

Guilt is not the sole preserve of parents though – guilt can occur as a result of a wide range of events. Perhaps you lost or broke something belonging to a friend or family member? Maybe you let someone down, said something derogatory or unkind.

Whatever it is, your perception of the events is that you think you did wrong and now you feel like crap! And the more you replay events over in your mind, the worse you seem to make them. It's like a game of Chinese whispers going on in your head: the more you replay it, the more distorted it becomes.

But hanging on to guilt serves no purpose. You have to forgive yourself. You can do that in the same way as you forgive someone else.

First, acknowledge, without exaggerating or minimizing what happened, the extent to which you were responsible. There may have been mitigating circumstances; you may have had no option but to do what you did; you may have been unable to get time off work to get to your child's school play; you may have been stressed when you made a critical remark; it may have been a complete accident that you broke something belonging to someone else.

You must, though, take responsibility for what you did. Don't seek to place blame elsewhere. Avoid, too, justifying what you did or pointing out the parts of the situation that you were not responsible for. Simply acknowledge the other person's pain without minimizing it, without excuses and without revisiting details of the situation.

On the other hand, although there may have been something you could have done differently, don't overestimate your responsibility. Don't exaggerate and dramatize and make it all about you!

Say sorry. A genuine apology can go a long way. Say what, specifically, you're sorry for. Are you sorry simply for not turning up or are you sorry that your friend felt so let down? Or is it both?

Now for the positive thinking: accept you did something wrong, but move on. What can you do or are you prepared to do, if anything, to make up for your actions?

If you are going to do something, make amends as soon as possible. Whatever it is, keep it in proportion to the wrongdoing. Missed your child's school play? Rather than make up for it by buying them a new computer game, spend time doing something nice together. And if you broke something belonging to someone else, get it fixed or replace it as soon as possible. Make it a priority.

Have hope that the other person will recognize your attempt to make amends but also be prepared for the fact that they might not be ready to do that just yet. If you've done what you can, accept that the ball is now in their court.

Regret

Closely related to guilt is the feeling of regret. Guilt arises from thinking and feeling you've done wrong. Regret arises from thinking and feeling that at some point in the past, you made a 'wrong' decision to do or not do something. With regret, you now see your action or inaction in a different light and feel that you have, in some way, lost out.

Regrets often start with the words 'I wish': 'I wish I'd been more patient', 'I wish I'd travelled more when I was younger', 'I wish I hadn't taken this job', 'I wish I'd ordered something else from the menu.' Regrets may also start with the words 'I should have'. 'I should have gone to university', 'I should have phoned.'

Regrets often focus on what you didn't do – the missed opportunities.

Unproductive regret (negative thinking) can paralyse you and leave you feeling defeated and hopeless. Productive regret (positive thinking) can help you behave differently in future.

Maybe you could or couldn't have done something then, but what are you in a position to do now?

'Stay away from what might have been and look at what can be.'

Marsha Petrie Sue

Acknowledge what did or didn't happen, accept that you can't change it and instead turn your thoughts to how to do things differently from now on:

* 'I wish I'd ordered something else on the menu *but now I'm going to ...*'
* 'I should've gone to university *but now I'm going to ...*'
* 'I should've phoned, *so instead, I'm going to ...*'

When you catch yourself thinking a regretful thought, add a positive thought to it. Remember the power of adding the word 'but' after a negative statement. (See Chapter 5.)

What you did or didn't do could either paralyse you further or motivate you to do something positive from now on. The only thing that keeps you stuck in lost possibilities is the refusal to focus on new ones.

But could you be holding back from moving forward because you fear failure?

In a nutshell

* Let go of expectations of how things 'should' be. It's too easy to remain disappointed if you're still attached to how things 'should' have been.

- Disappointment is actually helping you to move towards your goal, not away from it. You can learn from disappointments and move forward – sometimes in a different direction.
- Finding something positive in adversity doesn't mean denying how tragic and devastating the situation is, but it can help prevent you from being overwhelmed by the awfulness of it.
- Never put up with a bad, risky or harmful situation just because you can find some positive aspects to it.
- Identify the good things that can happen if you remove yourself from a potentially dangerous situation. By removing yourself, you put yourself in a positive position: one of being in control.
- Don't think that you can't be courageous because you don't *feel* courageous. Courage often requires that you act 'as if' you're confident, whatever you actually feel. It's feeling the fear and doing it anyway.
- Maybe there's something to learn from every criticism. Be willing to listen, decide if there's any truth in the criticism and act accordingly.
- Forgiveness means letting go of the resentment, frustration or anger that you feel as a result of someone else's actions. If you forgive someone, you don't change the past, you change the future.
- Hanging on to guilt serves no purpose. Accept you did something wrong, but move on. What can you do or are you prepared to do to make up for your actions?

- Regret arises from thinking and feeling that at some point in the past, you made a 'wrong' decision and that you have lost out.
- Acknowledge what did or didn't happen, accept that you can't change it and instead turn your thoughts to how to do things differently from now on.

8

Managing a Fear of Failure, Perfectionism and Comparing Yourself with Others

H ave you ever been afraid of failing at something and so decided not to try it at all? Not sure? Maybe then, at one time or another, you've *subconsciously* sabotaged an opportunity or an event in order to avoid failing at it.

Whether or not you're aware that you have a fear of failure, if you do, it's probably because you think you won't be able to cope with the disappointment, embarrassment and shame that can come with failing at something.

You might find some last-minute commitment or a minor physical problem – a headache or stomach ache – which you use as an excuse not to attempt something. Or if you do attempt it, in order to lessen your disappointment and avoid embarrassment if you fail, you might tell your-self – and other people – that you're unlikely to do well; that you don't expect to succeed. Although this can then increase the likelihood that you *will* fail (your negative thinking creates a self-fulfilling prophecy), your need to avoid failing at something is greater than your desire to succeed at it.

Having a fear of failure (atychiphobia) can, though, mean that you miss out in life. You might, for example, decline the opportunity to give a presentation at work in case you do badly and people think you're not up to the job. Or you might cancel going out on a date in case it's a disaster. But ducking out of the presentation because you fear that you'll fail could mean that you don't get offered any other interesting, career-enhancing opportunities in future. And pulling out of a date might mean you miss out on a good evening and a long-term relationship.

If you are often reluctant to attempt challenges and try new things, or you only ever get involved with activities and experiences that you know you'll succeed at, you may have a fear of failure. This can change! You can change the way you think and redefine the meaning of failure.

How to overcome a fear of failure

'Forget about the consequences of failure. Failure is only a temporary change in direction to set you straight for your next success.'

Denis Waitley

There are several things you can do to manage the unhelpful impact that a fear of failure can have.

Be aware of your thoughts, feelings and responses
The main problem with a fear of failure is that it tends to operate on an unconscious level. Think back to when

you've had an opportunity to achieve something – to learn something, for example, or visit somewhere new, to apply for a job, join a sports team, audition for a part or run a marathon. Did the thought of failing cross your mind? How did you feel about the prospect of not succeeding? What did you think? Did you think, for example, 'I'll never be good enough, so no point in going for it' or 'I'm not clever or talented enough'?

What did you do or not do as a result of your negative thinking? If you have a fear of failure, it's likely that you didn't follow through or that you sabotaged your chances in some way.

Fear of failure can cause you to consciously or unconsciously sabotage your chances of success, in a variety of ways. Perhaps you put off your involvement for so long – by failing to pay the deposit, sign up or submit the application – that it became too late to get involved.

Whatever you did or thought, if you now ask yourself: 'How did it help me to think like that?' the answer is obviously 'It helped me to avoid failure!' Fine. But right now, we're looking at how you can overcome that fear. So the appropriate question here is 'in what way was it *unhelpful* for me to think like that?' And the answer is likely to be that, one way or another, you missed out.

Change the way you think
You can choose to see the failure as a defeat; a waste of time and effort; proof of your inadequacy; the fault of outside circumstances; a disappointment and an

embarrassment. Or you can take a more positive approach and see failure as the learning experience that it most often is.

Rather than fear failure, recognize that if you do attempt something and fail, you can learn from it and put those lessons into practice the next time. So if, after a job interview, you fail to secure the job, you use the feedback to inform your next interview and increase the odds that you'll be successful next time. And if you attempt to make a birthday cake and it doesn't turn out as you'd hoped, then again, you can reflect on what you've learnt and use it to make a better cake next time.

Often, valuable insights come only after a failure. Just like the lessons learnt from disappointment, guilt and regret, the lessons learnt from failure are how you keep from making that same mistake again. Failure only stops you if you let it.

In everything you do, there's always a chance that you'll fail. Facing that chance, feeling the fear and doing it anyway, is not only courageous – but it opens you up to a range of opportunities.

In order to reduce the *fear* of failing, you can reduce the *possibility* of failing. If you're going to attempt something you failed at before, think about what you learnt from that. A driving test is an obvious example here. Whether it was a mock test or your actual test, if you failed a part of it, then naturally, you'd work on that part before attempting the test again. The same approach applies to everything else – think about what you learnt and what you'd do differently next time.

Reduce the possibility of failing   Set yourself up for success. As described in Chapter 3, whatever it is you would like to do and succeed with, identify your options, choose one of them as a way forward and then break that option down into small steps.

Create targets and goals that are relatively easy to achieve and think of achieving each small step as a series of small successes. Thinking and acting in this way really can prevent you from becoming overwhelmed by the fear of failing because you are only focusing on one relatively easy step at a time. You can visualize yourself doing well and achieving each step.

Have a contingency plan   If you're afraid of failing at something, having a 'Plan B' in place can help you feel more confident about moving forward. Think positively and recognize that switching to Plan B doesn't mean that you're giving up, it means that you're increasing your chances of success by recognizing there's more than just one way to achieve it.

Letting go of unhelpful perfectionism

Perfection is excellence. But is being a perfectionist the same as being a positive thinker? Well, if the self-talk of your inner perfectionist were cheering you on from the sidelines, that would be a good thing. But when the voice of your inner perfectionist is saying 'This isn't good enough, it's not right. It's not how it should be. It should be better than this', then it's not helpful and it's definitely not positive.

Maybe you want to challenge yourself to do well in something; to be the best and have the best. That's not a bad thing. But there's a difference between being an adaptable perfectionist and being an unadaptable perfectionist.

Adaptable perfectionism is all about developing and improving. It's a flexible approach; you adjust to accommodate changing conditions. Crucially, you recognize your limits and other people's and you don't stress yourself trying to perfect every little detail of something – your work, your appearance, an event etc.

Unadaptable perfectionists, on the other hand, are rarely satisfied with what they achieve. If something isn't perfect, they dismiss it. Unadaptable perfectionists rigidly conform to very high standards and expectations. They are unable to adjust to different conditions.

This sort of unhelpful perfectionism involves polarized 'all or nothing' thinking; there's no middle ground or grey areas. Things are either good or bad, a success or a total failure, clever or stupid. There's no room for adjustments, mistakes or imperfections.

If you are an unadaptable perfectionist you only see the negative aspects and focus on the relatively insignificant details of yourself, other people, experiences and events that are imperfect. And it bothers you that they're not perfect!

Often, just like people who fear failure, your self-worth is tied in to how well you achieve. But as you rarely live up to the high standards you set for yourself (and you might believe that others judge you on your ability to be perfect too), you fall into a downward spiral of self-criticism, guilt, blame and resentment.

By contrast, adaptable perfectionists acknowledge imperfections but don't get hung up on them. They have a broader perspective; they focus more on what is positive and good about themselves, other people, situations, etc. They see mistakes and difficulties as an opportunity to learn and imperfections as an opportunity to improve.

How to be an adaptable perfectionist
The key to healthy, adaptable perfectionism is in your expectations. So start by asking yourself, in what way is it helpful for me to think like this? In what way is it helpful to spend so much time and energy on making sure every aspect of something is perfect? If your demands and high expectations often leave you disappointed, upset or stressed, then clearly they're not helpful.

Nine times out of ten, perfectionists get hung up on the small details, needing every part of theirs or someone else's work, a social occasion, relationship, attitude or appearance etc. to be perfect.

But actually, it would be more be helpful to get some perspective and decide if, in the greater scheme of things, a particular aspect that's not perfect really does need so much time and attention. Perhaps all that time and attention could be better spent elsewhere.

So yes, the meal you made for friends last week was (almost) perfect but you were so stressed that you had a row with your partner and you were stressed and exhausted by the time everyone arrived.

Imagine how much better an occasion like that will be next time if, instead of fussing about getting the minor details absolutely perfect, you spend your time having a relaxing bath and an hour to yourself before your friends arrive.

'People throw away what they could have by insisting on perfection, which they cannot have, and looking for it where they will never find it.'

Edith Schaeffer

Go for good enough   Find a balance where you do your best but at the same time don't get caught up in trying to tweak, improve and perfect – or insist that someone else improves and perfects – each and every detail.

Will anyone really object if, for example, one course of that celebratory meal was bought at the supermarket instead of made by you? Will they be very disappointed if you don't have exactly the right candles, flowers, side plates or whatever it is that you're getting hung up about?

Think differently about what it means when things don't meet your high standards and expectations; when other people – colleagues and family members, for example – fail to do things as well as you.

Instead of focusing on what isn't perfect, focus on what aspects of the meal, party, job, relationship or someone else's efforts *are* good and good enough. Tell yourself to turn a blind eye to the imperfections. Force yourself to look for the positive aspects and focus on them.

Finally, bear in mind that whether you're making a celebratory meal, organizing your child's birthday party, decorating a room or preparing a presentation, whatever it is, when you are tense, stressed and stuck on insignificant details, you narrow your thinking and lose perspective.

You're more likely to do and achieve better when you can relax and enjoy what you're aiming for. Why set impossible standards that just create frustration and stress? When you are enjoying what you're doing, your perspective broadens, and you're more likely to focus on the positive aspects of the situation. It's a positive dynamic where one aspect positively influences another.

Comparing yourself with other people

'Comparison is the thief of joy.'

Theodore Roosevelt

We've all done it; we've all compared ourselves to others and gauged our own abilities, relationships, resources etc. on what we believe other people have and what they can do.

How often, though, do we compare ourselves with someone less fortunate than us and consider ourselves blessed? More often, we compare ourselves with someone who we believe to be better, or have better or more skills, abilities or personal qualities, and better or more resources and possessions. We compare ourselves with others in negative ways, comparing what we think is the worst of ourselves to the best we presume about others.

Comparing ourselves with someone else is an inaccurate and irrelevant measuring stick. It's a faulty comparison.

Take, for example, a quiet, calm and introverted person who likes to spend periods of time on their own (and feels there's something 'wrong' with them for this). What do they get by comparing themselves to a gregarious, outgoing person (who actually gets bored by an hour alone with themselves)?

What kind of illogical conclusions can result with this comparison? That the extrovert is better than the introvert? Of course not. Each individual has their own qualities and strengths but in different ways.

Comparing ourselves with others is one of the most insidious forms of negative thinking because there's no end to the possible number of comparisons you can make; there will always be something – or someone – else to compare yourself with. There's always someone you meet, see, listen to or read about that you can perceive as having more or doing better than you.

You may think that you're making a fair comparison between yourself and someone else but, in fact, confirmation bias prompts you to look for evidence to support and confirm what you've already decided is true; the negative ways in which you don't match up.

Because you already think that the other person is better than you in some way, and/or because you're feeling bad about what you do or don't have, you look for and accept evidence of what you don't have, can't do, will never be etc.

These sorts of negative comparisons add no value, meaning or fulfilment to your life. They only create resentment and a sense of unfairness and deprivation. You have nothing to gain, but much to lose.

Last year, Gina came to me for some career coaching sessions. She told me that reading her friends', family's and colleagues' social media posts recently, it seemed that everyone was doing better than her. Gina's younger sister had just announced that she'd been promoted to a management role. A colleague had posted pictures of a business trip to Europe. One friend had posted pictures of the house he'd just bought. Another had been accepted onto a Masters degree course. Two others had announced their engagements.

'I feel like such a loser,' everyone else is doing great things with their lives. I know I should be happy for them but it just gets me down when I realize how far behind I am compared to them.'

When I asked her what she meant about being so 'far behind' her friends, here's what she said: 'I'm 29 years old and I still haven't got into a management role. I haven't travelled anywhere on business. I don't earn enough to buy a house or even a decent car. I'm single and it seems like all my friends are either getting engaged or married. And to top it all, it's my school reunion this summer. Everyone's going to be talking about their great jobs, relationships, their travels and so on. I can't bear the thought of it.'

It's natural to want to know where you fit into the scheme of things. But measuring your worth, your abilities, opportunities, your career progress and so on with other people can only lead to feeling inferior.

You are too unique to compare fairly. Your skills, abilities, contributions and value are entirely unique to you and your purpose in this world. They can never be fairly compared to anyone else.

How, then, can you break free from comparing yourself in negative ways to other people? As I explained to Gina, comparing yourself to someone else puts focus on the wrong person. Your time and effort could be better spent thinking positively about yourself.

Once again, it helps to break free of the comparison habit if you ask yourself: 'In what way is it helpful for me to think like this?' Ask yourself too: 'in what way is it *unhelpful* for me to think like this?' If comparisons leave you feeling discouraged, demotivated and depressed, then clearly it's not helpful to think like this. Recognize that your thoughts are unhelpful. Let them go.

Move on to focusing on what you have done and are doing rather than what everyone else has done and is doing. Reflect on what you've experienced, achieved and/or overcome. See how far you have come.

Compare yourself with yourself. Go back to the exercise (in Chapter 6) where you were asked to identify your personal qualities. There will be qualities that you have ticked and unique reasons why you have those qualities. That's because you are unique. You're not a replica of someone else.

Even if you had a genetic twin, you would have grown up with different influences, experiences and choices. So how could your opportunities and achievements be the same? They couldn't. So try to see everyone, including yourself, as unique individuals with their own pasts and their own future potential.

Make a conscious effort to free yourself from comparisons and instead focus on your own qualities and pursue your own goals in your own way.

Compare less. Appreciate more

Turning your focus onto what you do have rather than what, compared to others, you don't have, is a far more positive direction to take. As suggested in Chapter 5, at the end of each day, think about what you have to appreciate and be grateful for. Getting into a habit of looking for what's going well in *your* life and the world around you helps to take the focus off others and what they have.

Remember, when you think about the positive events and people in your life, you groove those neural pathways that help to establish positive thinking as a habit.

Find inspiration without comparison

Comparing yourself with others is foolish. But finding inspiration and learning from others is wise. There's a difference.

Comparisons involve looking for what others have got and what you have not got. This can just leave you feeling discouraged and demotivated. Inspiration, on the other hand, involves being *motivated* by others' qualities and experiences. You feel encouraged to achieve, but according to your own abilities, skills and resources.

So, rather than compare yourself with others, think positively; see them as role models to learn from and inspire you rather than people who are 'better' or have more than you. And if you can't find a good role model, aim to be one!

In a nutshell

- Fear of failure arises from thinking you won't be able to cope with the disappointment, embarrassment and shame that can come with failing at something.
- Rather than fear failure, recognize that if you do attempt something and fail, you can learn from it and put those lessons into practice the next time. Failure only stops you if you let it.
- Perfectionists get hung up on the small details, needing every part of theirs or someone else's work, social occasion, relationship, attitude or appearance etc. to be perfect. Why set impossible standards that just create frustration and stress?
- Instead of focusing on what, in a situation, isn't perfect, focus on what aspects *are* good. Force yourself to look for the positive aspects and focus on them.
- Comparing yourself to someone else puts focus on the wrong person. Make a conscious effort to free yourself from negative comparisons and instead focus on your own qualities and pursue your own goals in your own way.
- Find inspiration without comparison. See other people as role models to learn from and inspire you rather than people who are 'better' or have more than you.

Conclusion

'Change your thoughts and you change your world.'
Norman Vincent Peale

So there you have it; the single most effective way to improve your life is to think positively.

And yet, if it's that simple, did you really need to read a whole book about it? Well, yes. Because now, having read this book, you'll find it easier to be a positive thinker. You'll now understand what positive thinking is and what it is not. You'll know how you can move from negative thinking to positive thinking and follow up your positive thoughts with positive action. You'll also know how to train your brain to think in positive ways and you'll understand the difference that positive thinking can make when you're going through difficult and tough times.

But now it's up to you; you have to make a conscious decision to think positively. You have to choose to think positively.

As Shakespeare wrote, 'Nothing is good or bad but thinking makes it so.'

Everything happens how it happens, and it's up to you to choose how you want to respond to it. It's up to you to find the good; to be positive regardless of what's happening around you.

You may be wondering, though, how long it takes to change a habit of negative thinking into a habit of positive thinking. Ten days? Three weeks? A few months? It's different for everyone; depending on our circumstances, we each become more positive at our own pace.

You can think of moving from negative to positive thinking as being rather like learning a new language while at the same time trying to stop using your native language. You don't expect to be fluent in your new language in a week or two and you don't expect your native language – negative thinking – to go away completely.

What you can expect, though, is that the more you use your new language – positive thinking – the more you will improve and the more you improve, the more likely you will be to use that language or think in that way again.

Remember the science: when you think or do something new, you create new connections – neural pathways – in your brain. Every time you repeat a behaviour or way of thinking, your brain uses those same neural pathways and they become stronger and deeper.

So, when it comes to thinking in a different way, just like using a new language, every time you practise using it you make it more likely that it will become your predominant way of thinking.

And if, for one reason or another, you find yourself slipping into negative thinking, just remember that all is not lost! It's amazing how quickly you can turn this around; you have a chance to practise positive thinking again every time you're aware that you need to do so.

As Oprah Winfrey said 'The greatest discovery of all time is that a person can change their future by merely changing their attitude.'

Choose a positive attitude!

Useful Websites

For positive, inspiring news, ideas and stories:

zenhabits.net
www.ted.com
www.ted.com/speakers/amy_cuddy
www.dailygood.org/
www.huffingtonpost.com/good-news/
www.goodnewsnetwork.org/
http://positivenews.org.uk/
www.sunnyskyz.com/

These organizations specialize in supporting anyone who is being bullied or abused.

If you are being bullied:

www.bullying.co.uk/
www.gov.uk/workplace-bullying-and-harassment

If you're a child or young person:

www.nspcc.org.uk
www.childline.org.uk

If you are a woman and need help and advice in cases of domestic abuse:

www.nationaldomesticviolencehelpline.org.uk/
www.womensaid.org.uk/
www.refuge.org.uk/

If you are a man and need help and advice in cases of domestic abuse:

www.mensadviceline.org.uk/mens_advice.php.html

If you are elderly or concerned about an older person being abused in some way:

www.ageuk.org.uk/health-wellbeing/relationships-and-family/protecting-yourself/what-is-elder-abuse/

About the Author

Gill Hasson is a teacher, trainer and writer. She has twenty years' experience in the area of personal development. Her expertise is in the areas of confidence and self-esteem, communication skills, assertiveness and resilience.

Gill delivers teaching and training for educational organizations, voluntary and business organizations and the public sector. She also works as a careers coach.

Gill is the author of the bestselling *Mindfulness Pocketbook* (2015) *Mindfulness* (2013), *Emotional Intelligence* (2014), the *Sunday Times* bestseller *How to Deal with Difficult People* (2015), *Overcoming Anxiety* (2016), *The Mindfulness Colouring and Activity Book* (2016) plus other books on the subjects of resilience, communication skills and assertiveness.

Gill's particular interest and motivation is in helping people to realize their potential, to live their best life! You can contact Gill via her website www.gillhasson.co.uk or email her at gillhasson@btinternet.com.

Index

Notes

Notes